C000256181

Forty Classic Cotswolds Pubs

"For lovers of good pub food and ale."

G. M. Ball
PukkaPubs.com

Forty Classic Cotswolds Pubs

Forty Classic Cotswolds Pubs
First Edition
Copyright © G. M. Ball
November, 2005

ISBN: 0-9551953-0-6

Cottage Ventures Limited

PukkaPubs.com is a wholly owned subsidiary of Cottage Ventures Limited.

PO Box 24
Stow-on-the-Wold
Cheltenham
Gloucestershire
GL54 1WX
England

Foreword

Have you ever licked your lips at the prospect of a sumptuous pub lunch, impeccably served, in surroundings fit for a king? And have you ever sat down to dine and been mortified to find stewed vegetables, sachets of salad cream, petulant adolescent service and a whining jukebox that you'd gladly pay to have turned off? If so, read on.

Welcome to the first edition of Forty Classic Cotswolds Pubs where you'll find the truth about wining and dining in these hostelries. I've had the good fortune to test, taste and drink in each of them and while I don't claim that these establishments are the best in the Cotswolds, I can vouch that they are all special nonetheless.

A word on geography. There is a green shaded area on 'Leisure Map 182 – The Cotswolds' and this ordnance survey data signifies this area as being of "Outstanding Natural Beauty" and it is within this area alone that I have surveyed the pubs for inclusion in this book. I strongly recommend buying a copy of the said map as finding some of these pubs could turn a perfectly nice afternoon into a rather frustrating one.

So what makes a great pub? Good beer, food, wine, ambience, service or clean toilets? Well, all of the above in my humble opinion. And I'm pleased to report that I did find such pubs in the Cotswolds and they were awarded three Silver Spoons. Alas, not all are worthy of such praise. Some have been awarded two Silver Spoons, others one and some none at all.

Before eating and drinking at any of the pubs, I kept it an absolute secret as to my real intentions for being there: to critique every move of the staff, every morsel of food placed upon the plate and each drop of liquid that went down the throat.

There is a formula for awarding the Silver Spoons contained in this book. It measures ambience, service, food and drink. But, just like the Coca-Cola recipe, I shan't be sharing the full details here. I do, however, strongly recommend that you take the 'Pukka Pubs' litmus test by visiting these fine establishments yourself.

If by chance I have omitted a rare gem, feel free to tell me by e-mailing the contact details below or returning the Feedback Form on Page 88 of this book. I do solemnly promise to get in my car (or walk if it is near to my house) and visit the said pub, and I do further promise that if I am in agreement with you, I will publish it in the next edition.

Lastly, to the best of my knowledge the information contained herein was correct at the time of going to print. Naturally, I cannot be held accountable for annoyances such as any of the establishments firing his/her chef and replacing them with a first-year cookery student from Gloucester Polytechnic.

Gastronomically yours,

G. M. Ball
lastorders@pukkapubs.com

Location of pubs

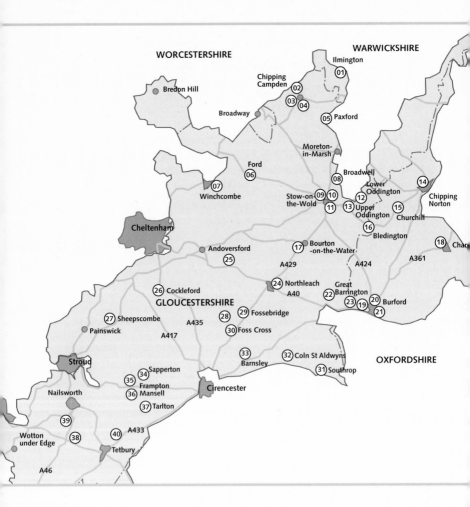

WARWICKSHIRE

WORCESTERSHIRE

Ilmington

(01)

Chipping
Campden (02)

Bredon Hill
(03) (04)

Broadway (05) Paxford

Moreton-
in-Marsh

Ford
(06)

Broadwell

(14)

(07) (08)
Winchcombe Stow-on- (09)(10) Lower
the-Wold (12) Oddington Chipping
(11) (13) Upper (15) Norton
Cheltenham Oddington Churchill
(16)
Bledington
(18) Cha
Andoversford Bourton
(17) -on-the-Water A361
(25)
A429 A424

Northleach
(26) Cockleford (24) A40 Great
GLOUCESTERSHIRE (22) Barrington
(23)(19) (20) Burford
(27) Sheepscombe (28) (29) Fossebridge (21)
Painswick A435
A417 (30) Foss Cross

(33) (32) Coln St Aldwyns OXFORDSHIRE
Stroud Barnsley
(35)(34) Sapperton (31) Southrop
Nailsworth (36) Frampton
Mansell Cirencester
(37) Tarlton

(39)

Wotton (38) (40) A433
under Edge Tetbury

A46

Contents

Other reasons to choose

Pubs with 3 Silver Spoons

02   The Noel Arms, Chipping Campden

15   The Chequers, Churchill

16   The King's Head, Bledington

31   The Swan at Southrop, Southrop

33   The Village Inn Pub, Barnsley

34   The Bell at Sapperton, Sapperton

40   The Trouble House, Tetbury

Pubs with a beer garden
(i.e. has grass, not patio)

01   The Howard Arms, Ilmington

03   Eight Bells, Chipping Campden

06   The Plough Inn, Ford

08   The Fox, Broadwell

12   The Fox Inn, Lower Oddington

24   The Wheatsheaf Inn, Northleach

25   The Puesdown Inn, Compton Abdale

27   The Butchers Arms, Sheepscombe

29   The Fossebridge Inn, Fossebridge

30   The Hare & Hounds Inn, Fosse Cross

35   Crown Inn, Frampton Mansell

36   The White Horse, Frampton Mansell

37   The Tunnel House Inn, Coates

38   The Gumstool Inn, Nr Tetbury

39   Tipputs, Nr Nailsworth

Note: Many pubs have patio areas where you can eat and drink, check individual pub reviews.

Pubs next to a river

22   The Fox Inn, Great Barrington

29   The Fossebridge Inn, Fossebridge

Pubs that do not allow children inside

18   The Bull Inn*, Charlbury

34   The Bell at Sapperton**, Sapperton

*No under fives.

**Allowed in the afternoon.

Pubs that do not allow dogs inside

01   The Howard Arms, Ilmington

02   The Noel Arms, Chipping Campden

05   The Churchill Arms, Paxford

13   The Horse and Groom, Upper Oddington

15   The Chequers, Churchill

17   The Old Manse Hotel, Bourton

18   The Bull Inn, Charlbury

27   The Butchers Arms, Sheepscombe

38   The Gumstool Inn, Nr Tetbury

Note: Many of the above allow dogs to be tied up outside. Best to phone ahead and check before arrival.

Notes

Five important things to remember when eating out

- Always book, then you'll never be turned away from a busy pub.

- If booking for lunch, double-check that it's not just bar snacks being served.

- Some pubs have different serving times depending on the season: check before you arrive.

- A good pub regularly changes its menu. If you're a fussy eater or minding your pennies, call ahead and see what's on offer.

- Check to see that the Landlord and Chef are the same as published in this book.

A word on walks

You will note that I have included 'Recommended Walks' at the end of most pub reviews. There are few better ways to build up an appetite or walk off a good lunch, than a relaxing stroll through the rich English countryside. My directions are not designed with GPS precision, but an investment of a few pounds in the excellent Ordnance Survey Cotswold Explorer OL45 will overcome any shortcomings in this area.

About the Author

G. M. Ball first visited the Cotswolds aged 19. He was immediately struck by the area's beauty, character and way of life. Eight years later he bought a house in a quiet corner of the Cotswolds that he now calls home. He took a two-year break from the stresses of life as a stockbroker in the City of London, and travelled the world where he worked in five-star hotels in Queensland, Australia, and leading restaurants in Vancouver, British Columbia, and Asia. He was a magazine publisher in Hong Kong, where he lived for 12 years before returning to his native England. His interests include travel, writing, photography, entrepreneurship, food, beer and wine, which, when all added together, equal this book. He is married and has one daughter.

The Howard Arms
ILMINGTON

Silver Spoon rating

Lower Green, Ilmington, Nr Shipston-on-Stour,
Warwickshire CV36 4LT
Tel: 01608 682226 www.howardarms.com

If a pub could reach out and put its arm around your shoulders to welcome you, The Howard Arms would be the Cotswolds' pub that would do it. Tucked into the northernmost reaches of the Cotswolds, its wall-crawling, blood-red English roses tell you you're about to be treated to a classic pub experience.

Two pleasing notices greet the eye as you enter: "This is a non-smoking pub throughout" and "Children should be seen and not heard after 7pm". This is a serious pub that attracts a serious clientele.

You can eat in the flagstoned floor area that surrounds the bar or the exquisite adjoining Georgian dining-room that manages to successfully bring the busy bar into its ambience.

The food itself is a sound mix of traditional and contemporary offerings and changes daily. The chefs are so proud of using almost exclusively local ingredients that they name all the suppliers and locations on a blackboard near the bar. When one says 'local', it is more a west-country flavour to the ingredients.

The evening I visited, the Cornish influence was well represented with grilled Cornish plaice and grilled Cornish sardines dusted in olive oil, making my party ignore the inviting beef in ale and mustard pie.

One area in which the Howard Arms lets itself down when you're dining is that you have to get drinks from the bar yourself. Remembering that this is a popular hostelry, a wait of five minutes at the bar is common, and rather defeats the object of ordering fresh sardines. Trays seem to be rare too, making the delivery of drinks to a table of six something akin to a juggling act.

The Howard Arms provides very good food in a beautiful setting; a drinks waiter would be an improvement and take nothing away from what's already there.

HOW TO GET THERE

In the centre of the village, a few miles off the A429 between Moreton-in-Marsh and Stratford-Upon-Avon.

TYPICAL MENU AND PRICES

Starters

Grilled Cornish Sardines – £6.00

Smoked Chicken and Avocado Rocket Salad – £5.50

Main Courses

Grilled whole Cornish Plaice – £14.00

Beef, Ale and Mustard Pie with Peppercorns – £9.50

Desserts

Pecan Buttered Tart – £5.00

Organic Sorbet – £4.50

RECOMMENDED WALK

The Centenary Way runs through the heart of Ilmington and connects with many footpaths with short and long loops back to the village. Glorious countryside in these parts.

Note: Use OS Explorer 205 for Ilmington.

? IMPORTANT FACTS

LANDLORD
Rob Greenstock

CHEF
Ray Boreham

BREWERY/FREEHOUSE
Freehouse

FOOD SERVING TIMES
Lunch: 12pm-2pm
Dinner: Mon-Thurs: 7pm-9pm,
Fri-Sat: 7pm-9.30pm,
Sun: 6.30pm-8.30pm

NON-SMOKING AREA
Yes - completely non-smoking

GARDEN
Yes

PARKING
Yes

CHILDREN WELCOME
Yes

DOGS ALLOWED
No

Noel Arms Hotel
CHIPPING CAMPDEN

Silver Spoon rating

High Street, Chipping Campden,
Gloucestershire GL55 6AT
Tel: 01386 840317   www.noelarmshotel.com

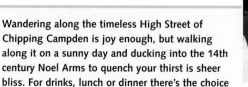

Wandering along the timeless High Street of
Chipping Campden is joy enough, but walking
along it on a sunny day and ducking into the 14th
century Noel Arms to quench your thirst is sheer
bliss. For drinks, lunch or dinner there's the choice
of a relaxed courtyard at the rear, a cosy non-smoking dining room or a good-sized
traditional bar that fronts onto the main street.

There are two things that stand out about the Noel Arms; the first is the excellent service.
The Singaporean Manager, Mr Loy, previously worked for five-star hotels, including The
Intercontinental in Mayfair. It's obvious he brings his national reputation for fastidiousness
and top-rated service skills to the table – literally. He works the tables with an easy
confidence and a personal charm that makes you feel your custom is genuinely
appreciated. Pub owners wanting to raise service standards should do no more than send
their staff for lunch here so they can understand what good service means.

The second thing that stands out, surprise, surprise, is the Asian cuisine served exclusively
in the evenings. All the classics appear on the menu including a range of curries,
Singapore noodles, spring rolls and sweet and sour chicken. For the Asian food
connoisseur there are pork dumplings (siu mai), Japanese udon soup and Indonesian
chicken rendang. Peer through the swing doors of the kitchen and you'll quickly see why
the food is so authentic and a delight to the taste buds: Sri Lankan Chef Indunil Upatissa
is assisted by a native Thai chef and an almost exclusively Asian team.

If Asian food isn't to your liking, lunchtimes have the usual British classics. The real ale on
offer includes the regular Hook Norton and her stronger sister, Hook Norton Coronation.

The Noel Arms is proof that when you get the right staff on the roster, magic is worked.

HOW TO GET THERE

On the B4035 between Evesham and Shipston-on-Stour.

TYPICAL MENU AND PRICES

Starters

Wok-fried Squid – £5.50

Vietnamese Spring Rolls – £4.95

Main Courses

Ceylon Seafood Coconut Curry – £12.50

Lemon Chicken – £10.50

Desserts

Coconut Soup – £5.50

Austrian Apple Strudel – £5.50

RECOMMENDED WALK

There are many fine walks around Chipping Campden. If you are attempting all 100 miles of the famous Cotswold Way to Bath, then the Chipping Campden War Memorial is the official start/finish point. Alas, if, as I suspect an hour's trundle is more to your liking, there are many short signposted loops over light rolling hills.

 IMPORTANT FACTS

 LANDLORD
Ian Taylor

 CHEF
Indunil Upatissa

 BREWERY/FREEHOUSE
Freehouse

 FOOD SERVING TIMES
Lunch: 12pm-2.30pm
Dinner: 6pm-9.30pm

 NON-SMOKING AREA
Yes - totally non-smoking restaurant

 GARDEN
Yes, small outside patio

 PARKING
Yes

 CHILDREN WELCOME
Yes

 DOGS ALLOWED
No

Eight Bells
CHIPPING CAMPDEN

Church Street, Chipping Campden, Gloucestershire GL55 6JG
Tel: 01386 840371
www.eightbellsinn.co.uk

People have been beating a path to the door of the Eight Bells for hundreds of years. During Henry VIII's reign the priests of nearby St James Church cleverly dug an underground tunnel the few hundred feet to the bowels of the Eight Bells to escape raids from his men and, probably, so they could also sneak quick halves between sermons! The Eight Bells is a quaint Cotswold pub; it's homely inside and there's a cobbled courtyard and garden at the rear that makes for a nice retreat on a summer's day or a starlit night.

Beer drinkers will be right at home here, the cask ales being excellent, varied and regularly changed. Heaven! For those who prefer wine, the list has been thoughtfully constructed with reasonable budgets in mind. There is also a refreshing list of fruit wines including Apricot, Damson, Sloe and Plum. There's even a small tapas menu if you just want a snack.

The main courses use fresh produce, but try too hard to be different and I felt the flavours in some dishes were lost in the complexity. The rice in my risotto had not been washed, making for a starchy starter and the dessert of dark chocolate tart served with a whole pear and strawberries and clotted cream was certainly a taste explosion, but more nuclear than firework. The service is just about okay, but the cosy surroundings call for something more friendly and intimate.

Campden's oldest inn is certainly worth a visit, but if you're in search of simple honest food then this probably isn't the place for you. Great place to throw your bicycle against the wall for a visit, but not a silver spooner.

HOW TO GET THERE
Just off the main High Street on the B4035 between Evesham and Shipston-on-Stour.

TYPICAL MENU AND PRICES

Starters

Tomato and Mozzarella Tartlet – £5.50

Smoked Mackerel and Apple Salad – £6.25

Main Courses

Grilled Whole Brixham Plaice – £14.95

Medallions of Peppered Tuna – £14.95

Desserts

White Chocolate and Raspberry Brûlée – £4.75

Rice Pudding with Rhubarb Compote – £4.75

RECOMMENDED WALK

See recommendation on page 11.

 IMPORTANT FACTS

 LANDLORD
Neil Hargreaves

 CHEF
Greg Sweet

 BREWERY/FREEHOUSE
Freehouse

 FOOD SERVING TIMES
Lunch: Mon-Thurs: 12-2pm,
Fri-Sun: 12-2.30pm
Dinner: Mon-Thurs: 6.30pm-
9pm, Fri-Sat: 6.30-9.30pm,
Sun: 7-9pm

 NON-SMOKING AREA
Yes - separate non-smoking
dining room

 GARDEN
Yes

 PARKING
No

 CHILDREN WELCOME
Yes

 DOGS ALLOWED
Yes (but only in the bar)

13

The Red Lion Inn
CHIPPING CAMPDEN

Lower High Street, Chipping Campden,
Gloucestershire GL55 6AS Tel: 01386 840760
www.redlionchippingcampden.co.uk

Silver Spoon rating

It might not be an original name, The Red Lion, but its imposing facade certainly gets your attention and draws you to the daily menu posted outside its arched stone doorway. You're not disappointed either with a suitably worn flagstoned main dining area hugging the bar, with a more private room for dining upstairs.

The food here is beautifully fresh, of a high quality and well presented. The menu is reassuringly compact with six starters and nine main courses, allowing Chef Rob Wylcox and his team to put everything into their offerings. Smoked salmon wrapped around honey-dressed leaves with lemon oil and dill revels in the creativity being fired up in the kitchen, while the celeriac and garlic soup shows this chef's sense of adventure. Despite this adventurous creativity, the chef makes sure it doesn't come at the expense of complementary flavours and textures.

Being a Greene King pub means, of course, that trusty Old Speckled Hen and IPA are served. An added bonus is that the father and son keepers of this ancient inn also stock a good cellar, with 40 wines to choose from, six of which are offered by the glass.

The service is fine with waiting staff knowing the menu well and confident enough to recommend food. The fierce competition for diners in Campden means the restaurant can be on the quiet side and therefore lacks a little in ambience on weekdays, but if you're simply looking for good food in very traditional surroundings, The Red Lion is excellent value.

HOW TO GET THERE

On the B4035 between Evesham and Shipston-on-Stour.

TYPICAL MENU AND PRICES

Starters

Soup of the Day – £3.95

Chicken Caesar Salad – £4.25

Main Courses

Wild Mushroom and White Truffle Oil Risotto
– £9.95

Rack of Cornish Lamb with Rosemary Garlic
Mash – £12.95

Desserts

Kalua and Bitter Chocolate Cheesecake – £5.65

Strawberries and Cream – £4.65

RECOMMENDED WALK

See recommendation on page 11.

IMPORTANT FACTS

 LANDLORD
Lawrence Taylor &
Andrew Taylor (Son)

 CHEF
Rob Wylcox

 BREWERY/FREEHOUSE
Greene King

 FOOD SERVING TIMES
Lunch: Mon-Thurs: 12-2pm,
Fri-Sun: 12-2.30pm
Dinner: Sun-Thurs: 6.30-
9.00pm, Fri-Sat 6.30-9.30pm

 NON-SMOKING AREA
Yes

 GARDEN
No

 PARKING
Yes

 CHILDREN WELCOME
Yes

 DOGS ALLOWED
Yes

The Churchill Arms
PAXFORD

Paxford, Chipping Campden, Gloucestershire
GL55 6XH Tel: 01386 594000
www.thechurchillarms.com

Silver Spoon
rating

This is another Cotswold pub that has built a loyal following amongst locals, and deservedly so. It has that unpretentious atmosphere that is warming and congenial, replete with low beams, fireplaces, and large open areas make for a feeling of space, whilst retaining that air of intimacy too.

The menu is changed daily and uses tasty local seasonal produce. This does mean that the menu can be limited. For example, there were no vegetarian options on the evening I visited. But a limited menu is only to be expected when using fresh, local and seasonal produce. A further benefit for the diner is that they use the homely idea of allowing you to choose from the range of fresh vegetables-of-the-day to mix and match and are included in the price of your main course. Local beetroot creamed and seasonal Jersey Royals went down perfectly.

You can sniff out a good chef by the salad dressing he makes and the steak that he serves. Alas, there was no salad on offer, so I chose steak. Sadly, it was a little tough, and the blue cheese on top was too mature and overpowered the flavour of the meat. My dining partner, however, enjoyed the delightfully tender chicken breast with mushrooms and risotto.

They serve a terrific pint of Moonlight here, as well as other local North Cotswolds beers. The wine list is interesting and varied, and suggests a particular interest in wines by the landlord. There are three to four wines by the glass and around twelve reds and twelve whites to choose from, should you be up for a bottle. The Churchill is what you expect a great local to be like and well worth the trek into this beautiful corner of the countryside.

HOW TO GET THERE
The only pub in the village. About five miles north-west of Moreton-in-Marsh on the A429.

TYPICAL MENU AND PRICES

Starters

Mushroom Soup – £4.00

Breast of Pigeon – £6.00

Main Courses

Chicken Breast with Mushrooms and Risotto – £12.00

Stuffed Pork Tenderloin with Olives – £11.50

Desserts

Warm Rice Pudding – £5.00

Fresh Fruit Salad – £3.50

RECOMMENDED WALK

The Diamond Way cuts through the centre of Paxford and taking its path north or south will allow you to pick up various marked footpaths that will lead you back to the Churchill for refreshments. Stunning countryside around here.

IMPORTANT FACTS

 LANDLORD
Leo Brooke-Little

 CHEF
David Toon

 BREWERY/FREEHOUSE
Freehouse

 FOOD SERVING TIMES
Lunch: 12-2pm
Dinner: 7-9pm

 NON-SMOKING AREA
Yes

 GARDEN
Yes

 PARKING
No

 CHILDREN WELCOME
Yes

 DOGS ALLOWED
No

The Plough Inn
FORD

Ford, Temple Guiting, Gloucestershire GL54 5RU
Tel: 01386 584215
www.theploughinnatford.co.uk

Silver Spoon rating

The beautiful hamlet of Ford is roughly between Cheltenham and Stow-on-the-Wold, and The Plough Inn is an excellent lunch-time retreat or destination following a pleasant evening drive during the summer. The food is good here and this pub has a deservedly strong following from locals.

This is horse country and there's not a lot of subtlety in reminding you. The large, well-kept beer garden overlooks a beautiful horse training circuit, while inside my fireside table displayed a photo of the majestic Desert Orchid coming home to win the Cheltenham Gold Cup in 1989.

You'll be as fast off the mark as a racehorse when your food arrives. I started with crispy coated whitebait, fresh as a morning gallop, while the half-shoulder of lamb with garlic and rosemary is cooked at a slow trot, much to its benefit. Typical desserts lean toward the classic, such as treacle tart, apple crumble and steamed jam sponge.

For landlords faced with petulant serving staff, a not-uncommon British malaise, you could take the Plough Inn solution and hire a squad of South Africans. Used to good service at home, the South Africans understand that paying good money rightly deserves efficient service in return.

The Inn is a short canter from the local Donnington brewery and it's fresh Donnington's that's on tap. The wine list is as unpretentious as the surroundings, if a little limited with only seven whites and seven reds to choose from. But don't let that put you off. The Plough Inn is a lovely little pub that deserves the great following it has built over the years.

HOW TO GET THERE
On the B4077 between Tewkesbury and Stow-on-the-Wold.

TYPICAL MENU AND PRICES

Starters

Crispy-coated Whitebait – £4.95

Walnut-crusted Brie – £4.95

Main Courses

Half-Shoulder of Lamb – £12.95

Green Thai Chicken Curry – £10.50

Desserts

Bakewell Tart – £3.95

Steamed Jam Sponge – £3.95

RECOMMENDED WALK

With Ford encircled by the Cotswold Hills, there are some cracking walks to be had. Be warned, however, this is hilly country. A Highland walker could hike these hills without drawing a deep breath, but the rest of us will need a reasonable level of fitness to make the most of this scenic area. The easiest option would be to join the Diamond Way that follows the path of the River Windrush for a mile or so to Temple Guiting.

(?) IMPORTANT FACTS

 LANDLORD
Craig Brown

 CHEF
Julian Davies

 BREWERY/FREEHOUSE
Donnington

 FOOD SERVING TIMES
Lunch: Depends on the season
Dinner: Depends on the season

 NON-SMOKING AREA
Yes

 GARDEN
Yes

 PARKING
Yes

 CHILDREN WELCOME
Yes

 DOGS ALLOWED
Yes (in the bar only)

The White Hart Inn
WINCHCOMBE

Silver Spoon rating

High Street, Winchcombe, Gloucestershire GL54 5LJ
Tel: 01242 602359
www.the-white-hart-inn.com

Without wishing to upset the wife, being served by Nicole Burr, daughter of the owner of the White Hart, makes you want to marry a Swede and eat smoked fish for the rest of your days. The proprietor's genuine welcome and warmth of the service always make even the best meal taste that much better.

Unsurprisingly, the food leans toward the Scandinavian variety with smorgasbords, lots of seafood and red meat. Fresh, generous helpings are presented with a consistently chic style that matches the light Nordic interiors. You could forget that this old pub stands in the shadow of ancient Sudeley Castle.

However, vegetarians will be disappointed, with not a single vegetarian option on the positively Viking menu. Shame. Wine lovers, on the other hand, will be joyous with no less than 40 wines on offer, ranging from Argentinean Chardonnay at £13.50 a bottle to St Julian Cru Exceptionalle 2000 at a Scandinavian-priced £50 a bottle.

There are some nice touches in this bistro-pub, that range from the complimentary salmon terrine and garlic butter served with warm bread, to the fresh cut flowers on each table.

Only small things stop this dining experience from being as 'exceptionalle' as the French Medoc in the cellar. The barman committed the cardinal sin of serving Old Speckled Hen in a John Smith's pint class. Tut, tut. More importantly, the tables are too close together to allow for intimate conversation. When in Winchcombe, however, this is the place to come.

HOW TO GET THERE

Six miles north of Cheltenham on the B4632, in the centre of Winchcombe.

TYPICAL MENU AND PRICES

Starters

Scandinavian Fish Platter – £6.95

Pan-fried Scallops in Orange Sauce – £7.95

Main Courses

Rack of Lamb – £14.95

Pan-fried Sea Bass – £13.25

Desserts

Lemon Posset – £4.95

Banoffee Pie – £4.95

RECOMMENDED WALK

Turn left outside the front door, walk past the Plaisterers Arms (try saying that after three pints) and turn left into Vineyard Street, which is a beautiful terraced row of houses that leads to the grounds of historic Sudeley Castle. Walk duration: 15 minutes to the Castle.

 IMPORTANT FACTS

 LANDLORD
David Burr &
Nicole Burr (Daughter)

 CHEF
Mikka Tuome

 BREWERY/FREEHOUSE
Freehouse

 FOOD SERVING TIMES
Lunch: Mon-Fri: 10-10pm
(bar food only), Sat-Sun: 11-
10pm (bar food only)
Dinner: Mon-Sun: 6-10pm
(A La Carte Menu)

 NON-SMOKING AREA
Yes

 GARDEN
No (patio at rear)

 PARKING
Yes

 CHILDREN WELCOME
Yes

DOGS ALLOWED
Yes (in the bar only)

The Fox
BROADWELL

The Green, Broadwell, Gloucestershire GL56 0UF
Tel: 01451 870909

The winding lane from Stow, with its flanking, rolling and undulating farm fields, work up a sense of anticipation and thirst, as you enter the quaint village of Broadwell. Set to one side of the expansive village green is the unpretentious Fox.

There's a strange sense of going back to the 1970s with the Fox, probably because the tied house's owner, Donnington Brewery, seems to think an ongoing 70s-theme to its pubs might somehow come back into fashion. Spending on décor seems as rare as a tuneful Bay City Roller. The danger of first impressions is that you might turn tail and run, but that would be a mistake.

The Fox is worth visiting for the friendly service, beautiful village setting, quaint garden at the rear and pub food that is, well, pub food. Like the décor, the pub sticks to a menu from the 70s too: the tried and tested scampi and chips, lasagna and cottage pie. But it does these dishes well. The lunch menu differs from the evening and is worth checking ahead if you're intending to book.

With the Donnington Brewery about a mile down the road, it makes a pint of Best all the more pleasing. A basic wine list conforms to the nuts and bolts style that is The Fox. If the weather's fine, there's a beer garden backing onto fields which give a sense of isolation in spite of being a mile from the busy market town of Stow.

You wouldn't come from far to visit the Fox, but if you're in the area with the children on a sunny day, The Fox will not disappoint.

HOW TO GET THERE
Turn left for Broadwell going southbound on the A429 between Moreton-in-Marsh and Stow-on-the-Wold. The only pub in the village.

TYPICAL MENU AND PRICES

Starters

Garlic Mushrooms – £4.25

Whole Whitebait – £4.25

Main Courses

Cheesy Cottage Pie – £7.50

Grilled Rib-eye Steak – £12.95

Desserts

Apple Pie with Ice Cream – £3.75

Treacle Sponge – £3.75

RECOMMENDED WALK

You can turn in any direction from the Fox and find yourself on a beautiful walk. But the best has to be a walk along Monarch's Way (which runs right through Broadwell) to Donnington Village and onto the incredibly picturesque Donnington Brewery via a connecting footpath and the Heart of England Way. One way: 40 minutes, return: double that. Warning: you can't buy a Donnington's at the brewery itself! Shame.

 IMPORTANT FACTS

 LANDLORD
Mike & Carol East

 CHEF
Mike East

 BREWERY/FREEHOUSE
Donnington

 FOOD SERVING TIMES
Lunch: Mon-Fri: 11.30-1.30pm, Sat: 11.30-2pm, Sun: 12-2pm
Dinner: Mon-Sat: 6.30-9.00pm

 NON-SMOKING AREA
Yes

 GARDEN
Yes

 PARKING
Yes

 **CHILDREN WELCOME**
Yes

 DOGS ALLOWED
Yes

The Queen's Head
STOW-ON-THE-WOLD

Silver Spoon rating

The Square, Stow-on-the-Wold,
Gloucestershire GL54 1AB
Tel: 01451 830563

You can't claim the Queen's Head is pretentious, but sitting on the majestic town square of this busy Cotswold town, it does look more like a tea-shop. As you enter, you're as likely to see a Labrador or a Yorkshire terrier perched on one of the pub's sofas, as you are to see one of the locals draining a glass of Donnington Ale, brewed just down the road.

The Queen's has quite a following from the locals and its location ensures tourists form a large part of the clientele, giving it an international ambience during the day. Crackling fires bring warmth to the Cotswold stone walls and flagstoned floors in winter and the open air of the small courtyard garden is available at the rear during summer.

No international food awards are likely to have been bestowed by the time you visit, but the food is good, basic, home-made fare. Unfortunately, if you have been to the Fox at Broadwell lately, it will bring a sense of déjà vu, with the menu sporting lasagna, vegetarian lasagna, scampi and chips and a host of eye-popping calorie-filled deserts such as hot chocolate sponge pudding, and bread and butter pudding.

Be aware that there's more chance of finding a boneless kipper in a blind-man's kitchen, than finding a parking slot during summer in Stow. But once parked beside the impressive inglenook fireplace with a pint you'll forget terriers, lasagna and tea-shops and bask in the feel of a real pub.

HOW TO GET THERE

Stow is mid-way between Cirencester and Stratford-upon-Avon on the A429. The Queen's is on Stow Square.

TYPICAL MENU AND PRICES

Starters

Soup of the Day – £4.00

Sizzling Garlic Mushrooms – £4.50

Main Courses

Trio of Cotswold Sausages with Herb Mash – £8.00

Home-made Chicken Pie – £8.00

Desserts

Hot Chocolate Sponge Pudding – £4.00

Bread and Butter Pudding – £4.00

RECOMMENDED WALK

Turn left outside the front door and after 20 paces take another left down a little alleyway. This will bring you onto the Fosse Way. Cross the road and walk down the short lane to open fields and follow the footpath signs down to the village of Lower Swell and have a pint of Donnington's Best at The Golden Ball.

Walk duration: 30 minutes to Lower Swell, 40 minutes back (up the hill).

 IMPORTANT FACTS

 LANDLORD
John Bate

 CHEF
June Cooke

 BREWERY/FREEHOUSE
Donnington

 FOOD SERVING TIMES
Lunch: 12-2.30pm
Dinner: Mon-Sat: 6-9.30pm

 NON-SMOKING AREA
Yes

 GARDEN
Yes

 PARKING
No

 CHILDREN WELCOME
Yes

 DOGS ALLOWED
Yes

The King's Arms
STOW-ON-THE-WOLD

The Square, Stow-on-the-Wold, Gloucestershire GL54 1AB
Tel: 01451 830364
www.kingsarmsstowonthewold.co.uk

**From the outside it looks as if the King's Arms
should reach across the square to the Queen's
Head, give it a good shaking and say, 'It was here
Charles 1st lodged in 1645. Clear off, usurper.'**

A glance inside through the mullioned window of
this coaching inn at night and you'd be forgiven for thinking you'd stumbled across a
worm-hole to Covent Garden.

This pub generated a strong following on the back of a Michelin-starred chef who
recently upped sticks and left to start his own bistro down the road. Luckily for Greene
King (the landlords), the new tenants are none other than the owners of the well-run
White Hart in Winchcombe (see page 20).

The same White Hart bistro-style is applied at this fine hostelry: fresh cut flowers, candles,
and before you can say "pint of Speckled Hen, please" a miniature bread board arrives
replete with olives and home-made bread.

Service attitude is better than under the previous tenant, but the food can't claim
Michelin stars (nor Silver Spoons). My mussels were lukewarm, gritty and smothered in
onions that would have been more suitably partnered with a fairground burger. And
Risotto served in the same bowl as a salad? Maybe it's a Scandinavian thing. A neatly
presented mocha chocolate box came and my spirits were momentarily lifted, but then
the tongue-curling taste of artificial cream brought me back down to terra firma with a
bang.

Nice place, nice people, but the food needs more love and passion infused into its core if
they want to pack this place out on a Friday night.

HOW TO GET THERE
Stow is mid-way between Cirencester and Stratford-upon-Avon on the A429.
The King's is on Stow Square.

TYPICAL MENU AND PRICES

Starters

Tomato and Mozzarella Salad – £5.50

Wild Mushroom Risotto (with Salad!) – £6.50

Main Courses

Baked Haddock with Caper Butter – £8.00

Baked Chicken Breast with Sweet Mash – £11.50

Desserts

Mocha Chocolate Box with artificial* Cream – £4.00

Strawberry Cheesecake with Basil Syrup – £4.00

added in by the Author

RECOMMENDED WALK

Turn left out of the front door, down Digbeth Street, pick up a few pocket-loads of pork pies at Langbourne's Butchers and continue on to the delightful village of Maughersbury. Follow the footpath all the way to the Fosse Way, turn right and walk back to the square in Stow and have a pint of Henry's at The Talbot in The Square. Walk duration: 45 minutes.

IMPORTANT FACTS

LANDLORD
David Burr

CHEF
Bjorn Moen

BREWERY/FREEHOUSE
Greene King

FOOD SERVING TIMES
Lunch: All day - bar snacks
Dinner: Mon-Thurs: 7-9.30pm
Fri-Sat: 7-10pm, Sun: 7-9pm

NON-SMOKING AREA
Yes - non-smoking restaurant

GARDEN
No

PARKING
No

CHILDREN WELCOME
Yes

DOGS ALLOWED
Yes (but only in the bar)

The Eagle and Child
STOW-ON-THE-WOLD

Silver Spoon rating

Digbeth Street, Stow-on-the-Wold, Gloucestershire
GL54 1BN Tel: 01451 830670
www.theroyalisthotel.co.uk

Legend has it that an eagle once adopted a small child and brought it up in its nest. Hence the name of this pub, also said to be the oldest in England and dating back to the 10th century.

As well as the oldest pub, it could also win a competition for the smallest bar in England too, with an area not much bigger or inviting than an industrial lift. This might have something to do with the fact that the two larger and airier rooms are only for dining. Thankfully, away from the world's smallest bar there is a rather delightful conservatory and the more traditional flagstoned, fireplaced main room that fronts the famous Sheep Street.

There's a daily specials board and a 'safe' English-focused menu. Braised lamb shank, washed down with a young South African Pinotage is pleasing. The fish and chips also received rave reviews from nearby diners, and the puddings are excellent and use seasonal fruit.

The service is good, with the waitresses wearing identical waist-high aprons with matching checked shirts. It's as if they've been on a 'get-the-waitressing-basics-correct' course and they've all passed with flying colours.

Claustrophobics should avoid coming for drinks only, but if you want a good lunch or dinner while basking in a millennium of history, then this pub does the job very well.

HOW TO GET THERE

Stow is mid-way between Cirencester and Stratford-upon-Avon on the A429.
The Eagle and Child is on Digbeth Street, just off Stow Square.

TYPICAL MENU AND PRICES

Starters

Royalist Fish Cakes – £4.95

Crispy Duck Spring Rolls – £5.75

Main Courses

Chargrilled Tuna with Nicoise Salad – £12.99

Supreme of Chicken, Mash in Mushroom and
Tarragon Sauce – £10.99

Desserts

Raspberry and Lemon Pavlova – £4.50

Dark Chocolate Tart with Orange Sorbet
– £4.99

RECOMMENDED WALK

Go left outside the front door, walk five paces
and turn left again onto Park Street and walk to
the end of the road. You'll come to Well Lane
that overlooks beautiful countryside. Keep
walking less than half-a-mile and you'll come to
Stow Well, an ancient natural spring. Fitter
walkers can walk on to Broadwell and the
quaint Fox Inn.

 IMPORTANT FACTS

 LANDLORD
Niche Group of Hotels

 CHEF
Mark Coleman

 BREWERY/FREEHOUSE
Freehouse

 FOOD SERVING TIMES
Lunch: 12-2.30pm
Dinner: 6-9.30pm

 NON-SMOKING AREA
Yes - non-smoking restaurant

 GARDEN
No

 PARKING
No

 CHILDREN WELCOME
Yes

 DOGS ALLOWED
Yes

The Fox Inn
LOWER ODDINGTON

Lower Oddington, Gloucestershire GL56 0UR
Tel: 01451 870555
www.foxinn.net

Silver Spoon rating

The long line of cars leading up to The Fox Inn on a Thursday lunchtime is a sure indication of this pub's popularity. It's easy to see why, as the food is excellent and the cosy interior has 'classic country pub' written all over it. Unfortunately, this quaint inn has become a victim of its own success, as the sheer volume of people eating here makes for very patchy service.

Despite some reticence on service, The Fox Inn still picks up two Silver Spoons for the sheer quality of food and the abundant Cotswold ambience within this 16th century inn. The freshest of ingredients are fused with a deft use of herbs, ensuring the steaming hot delivery of pub classics such as braised lamb shank with rosemary red wine. Other dishes recommended by regular diners include honey and mustard-baked ham with parsley sauce. I'd highly recommend the prawn and saffron risotto.

Behind the bar are well-kept local ales including Arkells and Hook Norton. The wine list is extensive, although a little too heavily French. Wine prices start at £17.50 for a Chilean Merlot and bubble up to £39.50 for a white Burgundy from Domaine Philippe Chavy. No less than nine wines are offered by the glass.

There is a charming garden that comes alive in summer and the walks around this area are among the best in the Cotswolds. If the Fox Inn can reinvest some of its profits in more staff to cope with its popularity, this pub could be among the best in the land.

HOW TO GET THERE
Take the A436 from Stow and turn right after two miles into Lower Oddington.
The only pub in the small village.

TYPICAL MENU AND PRICES

Starters

Soup of the Day – £3.95

Smoked Salmon with Shaved Fennel – £6.95

Main Courses

Home-made Beef Steak and Kidney Pie – £9.50

Lasagna with Roasted Peppers – £8.25

Desserts

Crème Brûlée – £4.50

Chocolate Brownie with Clotted Cream – £4.50

RECOMMENDED WALK

The MacMillan Way snakes its way through Oddington, giving the walker a number of options. My preference would be to pick up the Bridleway that leads a few miles to the award-winning organic shop at Daylesford Organic Farm. Keener walkers can pick up the Diamond Way here, which takes you on a neat loop back to the MacMillan Way through the beautiful Daylesford Estate.

 IMPORTANT FACTS

 LANDLORD
Ian Mackenzie

 CHEF
Ray Pearson

 BREWERY/FREEHOUSE
Freehouse

 FOOD SERVING TIMES
Lunch: 12-2pm
Dinner: Mon-Sat: 6.30-10pm,
Sun: 7-9.30pm

 NON-SMOKING AREA
No

 GARDEN
Yes

 PARKING
Yes

 CHILDREN WELCOME
Yes

 DOGS ALLOWED
Yes

The Horse and Groom
UPPER ODDINGTON

Silver Spoon rating

Upper Oddington, Moreton-in-Marsh, Gloucestershire
GL56 OXH Tel: 01451 830584
www.horseandgroom.uk.com

This is your classic country pub in a setting that makes it hard to pass by in the car and would be a crime to do so if you're on foot. The interior has been completely modernised but retains all the old beamed features. It's a homely place, chopped wood beside two delightful fireplaces, comfy fireside chairs with a range of newspapers and magazines to read while cherishing a pint of Hereford Pale Ale or a glass of Sauvignon Blanc.

Come here during the week and its modernity might make you feel the pub is a little bare, but come at the weekend: you'll be hard pushed to get a table and the place comes into its own.

The food sticks to tried and tested classics such as home-made soups, fish pie, steaks, and fish and chips, doing a proper job with all. The service is friendly and helpful, but on the day I visited a few after-work English lessons for the waitress would have come in handy to speed up the communication.

Ales include the trusty Hook Norton and regular guest ales. The wine list is comprehensive and the bar staff are friendly, helpful and efficient. This is a good pub with good fare and makes for a perfect stopping-point en route through the North Cotswolds or as an easy side trip from Stow-on-the-Wold.

HOW TO GET THERE
Take the A436 from Stow and turn right after two miles into Upper Oddington. The only pub in the small village.

TYPICAL MENU AND PRICES

Starters

Goats Cheese and Chargrilled Vegetable Terrine
– £5.95

Soup of the Day – £4.75

Main Courses

Roast Breast of Chicken wrapped in Bacon
– £13.50

8oz Sirloin Steak with Fine Green Beans and
Shallots – £16.50

Desserts

Orange Panacotta – £5.50

Blueberry, Honey and Almond Tart – £6.00

RECOMMENDED WALK

Turn left outside the front door and walk
through the village and into Lower Oddington
to sniff out The Fox Inn.
Journey time: 15 minutes.

IMPORTANT FACTS

 LANDLORD
Sally & Simon Jackson

 CHEF
Jason Brewster

 BREWERY/FREEHOUSE
Freehouse

 FOOD SERVING TIMES
Lunch: 12-2pm
Dinner: 6.30-9.30pm

 NON-SMOKING AREA
Yes

 GARDEN
Yes (patio area)

 PARKING
Yes

 CHILDREN WELCOME
Yes

 DOGS ALLOWED
No

The Chequers
CHIPPING NORTON

Goddards Lane, Chipping Norton, Oxfordshire OX7 5NP
Tel: 01608 644717
www.chequers-pub.co.uk

This is the pick of the pubs in Chipping Norton, serving excellent Fullers Ale, good food and seventeen wines by the glass, and all in traditional 15th century surroundings. What could be better?

Beer-lovers will be right at home here, with the full range of Fullers Ales including the excellent newcomer to the family, Discovery, light in colour but full in taste. Parking is a drag in 'Chippy', as the locals call it, so if you can manage somehow to not drive, so much the better.

There's a covered courtyard that might be a little on the modern side for some or a fabulous example of how to mix new with old for others. It manages to close out the buzz of this busy Inn, letting in plenty of light and making the best place to eat.

Daily blackboard specials are popular and change according to what's in season. I plumped for the piping hot tomato and basil soup which came with garlic bread on the side and was excellent. For my main course I had mixed seafood over noodles and though the noodles were overcooked, the seafood and light sauce were delightful.

The landlords are very professional in their approach to quality and service here and the local staff show a friendly and courteous service. If in Chippy, this is the place to come.

HOW TO GET THERE
Chipping Norton is midway between Evesham and Oxford on the A44. The Chequers is down a small road that leads off the High Street.

TYPICAL MENU AND PRICES

Starters

Tomato and Basil Soup – £3.95

Chicken Caesar Salad – £4.95

Main Courses

Chicken Thai Green Curry – £8.95

Garlic Roasted Rack of Lamb – £11.95

Desserts

Vanilla Crème Brûlée – £3.95

Sticky Toffee Date and Pecan Pudding – £3.95

RECOMMENDED WALK

There are a number of footpaths leading out of Chippy. Light walkers can use them to head south to Churchill, where you can have refreshments by a pub of the same name (see Pub 15). Alternatively you could drive to the nearby quaint 150-year-old Hook Norton brewery, take a tour, buy a case of ale (if you have a horse with you) and then follow the footpath to the village of Great Rollright and loop back. Both round-trip walks will take you about an hour.

Note: Use OS Explorer 191 for Chipping Norton.

 **IMPORTANT FACTS**

 LANDLORD
Josh & Kay Reid

 CHEF
Brian Arnold

 BREWERY/FREEHOUSE
Fullers

 FOOD SERVING TIMES
Lunch: Mon-Sat: 12-2.30pm, Sun 12-5pm
Dinner: Mon-Sat: 6-9.30pm

 NON-SMOKING AREA
Yes - in restaurant

 GARDEN
No

 PARKING
No

 CHILDREN WELCOME
Yes

 DOGS ALLOWED
Yes

The Chequers
CHURCHILL

Church Road, Churchill, Oxfordshire OX7 6NJ
Tel: 01608 659393

Silver Spoon rating

You could see this place confusing our own World War II leader on his summer holidays and after a rather good lunch. But at the weekend a couple of dozen pairs of muddy boots at the oak front door might give it away. If thirsty walkers strolling around the bar in socks upsets your sensibilities, then avoid The Chequers. On the other hand if you rate empty welly-boots as an indicator of the bounty of the countryside that surrounds this picturesque Oxfordshire village, then take a visit.

The trio of Asumpta, her partner Peter and the chef Patrice Rogers have used a formula that previously worked well at the Horse and Groom at Upper Oddington. Everything from the genuine warm welcome, to the attention to detail of the well-trained staff, makes this pub work like clockwork. The contemporary feel of the bar and restaurant, with high beamed ceilings, modern lighting, new flagstones and light wooden furniture makes eating inviting and relaxed. But it is the pure genius of the food that makes a trip to Chequers a delightful experience.

Dishes, such as whiskey-marinated venison and crispy duck in pink peppercorn sauce, show the chef's sense of pleasure and creativity in his art. Yet Asumpta's business sense ensures that firm favourites like fillet steak, and timeless dessert classics such as apple and rhubarb crumble with custard, or rice pudding with brandy-stewed plums, are always on offer.

The beers are changed regularly, but there's almost always Hook Norton on tap. The wine selection, although varied, with nine whites, ten reds and a rose, will not excite the wine connoisseur. Considering the standard of the food, this should be rectified post haste, but this is a minor misgiving. A trip to Chequers is sheer joy and recommended to anyone who finds solace in great cooking in a traditional setting, without costing the earth.

HOW TO GET THERE

Three miles south-west of Chipping Norton on the B4450. The only pub in the village.

TYPICAL MENU AND PRICES

Starters

Chequers Salad with Duck, Smoked Chicken – £6.00

Smoked Haddock Kedgeree – £6.00

Main Courses

Fillet Steak with Provencal Tomatoes and Sautéed Mushrooms – £16.00

Grilled Sea Bass with Asparagus in Hollandaise Sauce – £13.50

Desserts

Apple and Rhubarb Crumble – £4.50

Rice Pudding with Brandy Stewed Plums – £4.50

RECOMMENDED WALK

There's an imposing church opposite Chequers which is worth a visit. There are also a number of walks that will take you in any direction you wish to choose. The walks westwards toward Stow offer fine views as the sun is setting.

 IMPORTANT FACTS

 LANDLORD
Peter Golding &
Asumpta Monaghan

 CHEF
Patrice Rogers

 BREWERY/FREEHOUSE
Freehouse

 FOOD SERVING TIMES
Lunch: Mon-Sat: 12-2.00pm,
Sun: 12-3.00pm
Dinner: 7-9.30pm

 NON-SMOKING AREA
Yes

 GARDEN
No

 PARKING
Yes

 CHILDREN WELCOME
Yes

 DOGS ALLOWED
No

The King's Head
BLEDINGTON

Silver Spoon rating

The Green, Bledington, Oxfordshire OX7 6XQ
Tel: 01608 658365
www.kingsheadinn.net

The King's Head is the sort of pub you would invent if it did not exist. Sat upon the village green, meandering brook at its side, this pub is a polished gem, and a place that will linger in the memory long after the experience has passed.

Pushing open the thick oak door you enter a world of low beams, crackling fires, friendly banter from the locals and the unmistakable smell of home cooking. It's the sort of olde worlde bar you'd expect, with amiable bar staff and a drooling array of beers. There are several guest ales to keep you happy while you mull over the latest offerings from head chef, Charlie Loader, chalked on the blackboard.

Charlie decamped from London's Leicester Square to Bledington in September 2003. He manages to combine an inventive range of food with the simple and classic like fish pie, and Gloucester Old Spot sausages. There is a large selection of vegetarian dishes all thoughtfully presented and even a kids' menu. It's boasted that the vegetables often come from the gardens of the locals that drink in the pub.

You can eat at the bar (my preference) or in the purpose-built restaurant attached to it. There is also an area for adults with children, so that the little ones can squeal to their heart's content while not annoying those in search of refuge. The King's Head gets a rare 3 Silver Spoon rating for its superb ambience, exceptional cooking, fresh ales and good wine list, all attentively served by friendly and well-trained staff.

HOW TO GET THERE

The only pub in this village. Take the A436 from Stow, and then turn right after 1 mile onto the B4450.

TYPICAL MENU AND PRICES

Starters

Soup of the Day – £4.00

Seared Tuna, Crispy Leeks with Ginger & Soy Sauce – £6.75

Main Courses

Smoked Haddock and Chive Fishcakes – £10.50

Ham, Leek and Mushroom Pie – £12.50

Desserts

Coffee and Walnut Cake with Cappuccino Ice Cream – £4.75

Raspberry and Kia Mousse – £4.75

RECOMMENDED WALK

There are plenty of walking options around Bledington. The Oxfordshire Way cuts through the heart of Bledington and runs beside the beautiful St Leonards Church. My recommendation would be to head west toward Westcote and pick up the Diamond Way to Icomb, one of the Cotswolds' most picturesque villages. A footpath will lead you back to Bledington. Round trip: A little over an hour.

? IMPORTANT FACTS

 LANDLORD
Archie & Nicole Orr-Ewing

 CHEF
Charlie Loader

 BREWERY/FREEHOUSE
Freehouse

 FOOD SERVING TIMES
Lunch: 12.00pm-2pm
Dinner: 7.00pm-9.30pm

 NON-SMOKING AREA
Yes

 GARDEN
Yes

 PARKING
Yes

 CHILDREN WELCOME
Yes

 DOGS ALLOWED
Yes

The Old Manse Hotel
BOURTON-ON-THE-WATER

Victoria Street, Bourton-on-the-Water, Gloucestershire GL54 7BX
Tel: 01451 820082
www.oldmansehotel.com

Despite having the stench of a pub chain about it,
I could not help but include The Old Manse in this
book because my pint of Old Speckled Hen was
simply the best I've had. The service was
especially good and by the end of my third
Cumberland Sausage I wished there was a fourth, such was their freshness and taste.

Gastronomic pub, however, this is not. The menu is among the most limited I've seen anywhere, with only seven main courses to choose from (one of these being that family-favourite chicken liver with onions!). In an effort to reach for haute cuisine, some of the other offerings were over-complex: quite how chicken, bacon and mangoes go on the same plate, I am not sure. Equally, I'd be curious to know how many punters order melon with candied orange and ginger for starters.

But this is a good pub to bring the family. The lunchtime menu includes a range of fresh baps, baked potatoes and favourites such as scampi, and bangers and mash. Other plus points include a children's menu, which has almost as many choices as the adults' menu, a non-smoking restaurant and, a huge plus: the pub's delightful riverside setting means you can feed the ducks afterwards as well.

Worth a visit if you're in the area but the chef needs to invest in a blackboard and some chalk, and get creative each morning to build a loyal following from foodies.

HOW TO GET THERE

On the A429 between Northleach and Stow-on-the-Wold and sat alongside the River Windrush.

TYPICAL MENU AND PRICES

Starters

Tomato, Mozzarella and Basil – £3.95

Seafood Linguine – £5.25

Main Courses

Grilled Trout with Mushrooms – £8.95

Sirloin Steak and Chips – £11.95

Desserts

Chocolate and Grand Marnier Mousse – £3.45

Honey Crème Brûlée – £3.45

RECOMMENDED WALK

Bourton is blessed with walks in all directions. One of the locals' favourites is the few miles along the Heart-of-England Way, to picturesque Lower Slaughter. Keener walkers can continue on to her other half, Upper Slaughter. Once there, there are a number of options to bring you back to your starting-point.

 IMPORTANT FACTS

 LANDLORD
Gill & Keith Ashburne

 CHEF
Louise Walters

 BREWERY/FREEHOUSE
Greene King

 FOOD SERVING TIMES
Lunch: 12.00pm-2.30pm
Dinner: 6.00pm-9.00pm

 NON-SMOKING AREA
Yes

 GARDEN
Yes

 PARKING
Yes

 CHILDREN WELCOME
Yes

 DOGS ALLOWED
No (but allowed in garden)

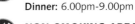

The Bull Inn
CHARLBURY

Silver Spoon rating

Sheep Street, Charlbury, Oxfordshire OX7 3RR
Tel: 01608 810689
www.bullinn-charlbury.com

The Bull Inn on Sheep Street is the heart of this small town. The locals use it like another sitting room, taking the dog, newspapers and children along to enjoy the homely surroundings, good pub food and lip-smacking and regularly changed guest ales.

Run by the Ludden family, including their two daughters, there's a distinct family and community feel to the 16th century Bull which is both welcoming and warming, and ensures service is always good. You can eat in the bar or in the cosy flagstoned, oak-beamed dining area. There's a bar snack menu listing the usual pub suspects and a more imaginative a la carte menu in the main restaurant, which is a tad twee for my tastes.

Local produce is a feature which the proprietors pride themselves on and hence the menu changes regularly. Year-round dishes include fish and chips which is particularly good, as are the home-made puff pastry pies. Leave room for desserts – there are a number of excellent classical choices including sticky toffee pudding, and apple and blackcurrant crumble.

I would recommend the Bull for either a quick bite in the bar and a pint of Hook or for a family celebration accompanied by a few bottles of wine from the well-priced wine list.

HOW TO GET THERE

Between Chipping Norton and Woodstock. Leave the A44 and join the B4022, The Bull is in the centre of this small town.

TYPICAL MENU AND PRICES

Starters

Oak-smoked Scottish Salmon – £6.25

Breaded Butterfly King Prawns with Chilli Dip – £5.75

Main Courses

Tarragon Breast of Chicken – £10.50

Smoked Haddock Florentine – £10.50

Desserts

Sticky Toffee Pudding – £4.25

Apple and Blackcurrant Crumble – £4.25

RECOMMENDED WALK

Light walkers can go south-east via footpaths to nearby Wychwood Forest and loop back to Charlbury. Duration: one hour. Walkers wanting to work off more calories than they've taken on over lunch could walk along the Oxfordshire Way (which cuts through Charlbury) to Blenheim Palace (distance: approx 5 miles). In a small churchyard, in nearby Bladon, is a piece of land that will be forever England and there lies Sir Winston Churchill.

Note: Use OS Explorer 180 for Charlbury.

 IMPORTANT FACTS

 LANDLORD
Gerard & Val Ludden

 CHEF
Gerard Ludden

 BREWERY/FREEHOUSE
Freehouse

 FOOD SERVING TIMES
Lunch: Tues-Sat: 12-2pm,
Sun: 12-2.30pm
Dinner: Mon-Sat: 7-9pm

 NON-SMOKING AREA
All non-smoking

 GARDEN
Yes, small courtyard

 PARKING
Yes

 CHILDREN WELCOME
No under 5's

 DOGS ALLOWED
No (but welcome on the courtyard)

The Lamb Inn
BURFORD

Silver Spoon
rating

Sheep Street, Burford, Oxfordshire OX18 4LR
Tel: 01993 823155
www.lambinn-burford.co.uk

You can't help but fall in love with Burford. The
street, on which The Lamb Inn has stood for a
half-millennium, is one of the finest examples of
Cotswolds' architecture that you are likely to find.
Pull the sofa in front of a roaring fire here in
mid-winter, sit down under the crooked beams with a bowl of soup and a bottle of red
wine, and all seems well in life.

The pub has two choices of place to eat: the much less formal bar area and the rather
grand dining-room. There's a bar menu and a fixed-price two- or three-course restaurant
menu. The dining room with its chandeliers, antique furniture, fresh cut flowers, carefully
choreographed red and white decor and correct table settings, is best for a celebration,
while the bar is a better bet for an informal weekend lunch or dinner.

The chefs take food here very seriously and diners in search of gammon steak with
pineapple chunks will be gravely disappointed. Everything from the inventive individual
menus, to food presented as if the chef's life depends on it, makes The Lamb Inn a class
act.

I dined in the Lamb's main dining room for a celebration and I can personally recommend
the fillet steak, the risotto and the chocolate mousse. There is a rustic elegance in the
food that's not easily found. On the drinks side of the equation the wine list is
complementary and there's always trusty Hook Norton on tap.

Although the staff are helpful and mostly friendly, they are a smidgen too formal and this
creates a whiff of snobbishness that, along with the dining-room, may put a few people
off. But don't let this spoil a visit. If your budget allows, the food and the beautiful setting
justifies a trip to The Lamb any day of the week.

HOW TO GET THERE
On the A40 between Oxford and Cheltenham. Turn into Burford High Street and then
turn left half way down the High Street into Sheep Street. Follow your nose.

TYPICAL MENU AND PRICES

Note: Two courses cost £29.50 and three courses cost £32.50

Starters

Spinach Soup with Shallot Crème Fresh

Ham-hock Terrine

Main Courses

Slow-cooked Fillet of Beef with Chive Pomme Puree

Pan-fried Halibut with Basil Mash

Desserts

Mango Doughnuts with Chilled Mango and Chilli Soup

Lemon and Lime Cake with Lime Sorbet

RECOMMENDED WALK

There aren't as many walking options around Burford but it is blessed with the River Windrush running through its northern end. Walkers can head east along the river toward Swinbrook and follow a combination of bridleway and footpath back to Burford via Fulbrook. A large lunch may be in order as the distance covers around six or seven miles.

 IMPORTANT FACTS

 LANDLORD
Michael & Pamela Horton

 CHEF
Shaun Dulce

 BREWERY/FREEHOUSE
Cotswolds Inns & Hotels

 FOOD SERVING TIMES
Lunch: Mon-Fri: 12-2.30pm, Sat-Sun: 12-3pm
Dinner: 6.30-9.30pm

 NON-SMOKING AREA
Yes (restaurant entirely non-smoking)

 GARDEN
Yes

 PARKING
No

 CHILDREN WELCOME
Yes

 DOGS ALLOWED
Yes (but not in the restaurant)

The Mermaid Inn
BURFORD

**High Street, Burford, Oxfordshire OX18 4QF
Tel: 01993 822193**

The Mermaid Inn, appropriately enough, is next door to the fishing-tackle shop. Not only that, but it serves a sea-food risotto that Rick Stein would be proud of. The freshest mussels, prawns and crab are delivered in a saucy risotto that will have you rushing back to Burford. The fish and chips are also exquisitely battered and fresh every day.

Despite some wonderful cooking, there are some extraordinary culinary gaffes to go with it. The free side-salad, for example, looked like a competition to see how many vegetables the chef could get into one bowl at the same time. There's also an off-putting service-lift system for the food which gives you the impression that it's been hoisted from a local building site. The lift brings steaming hot food up from the bowels of the building and sends soiled cutlery, plates and leftovers back down. Nice.

Yet The Mermaid somehow gets away with these faux pas. It's housed in an ancient building on one of England's most beautiful streets and the interior has a homely and laid-back feel with candles on each table, mood lighting, polished floorboards and an airy conservatory at the rear.

The menu is a combination of traditional fare such as steak and ale pie, fish and chips, and sirloin steak, and creative cuisine that includes warm dressed crab in a creamy brandy sauce and warm griddled salmon topped with melted goat's cheese.

The Mermaid is a curious place. The cooking has flashes of brilliance, the ambience is pleasing but not a delight, the service is fine but delivered with no passion. A little more tender loving care and The Mermaid could become a place you would go back to for more than just the risotto, and fish and chips.

HOW TO GET THERE
On the A40 between Oxford and Cheltenham. Turn into Burford High Street and The Mermaid is half way down on the left hand side.

TYPICAL MENU AND PRICES

Starters

Chicken Liver and Wild Mushroom Terrine – £6.00

Soup of the Day – £4.50

Main Courses

Steak and Ale Pie – £10.00

Whole Lemon Sole – £12.00

Desserts

Chocolate Nut Brownie – £4.50

Orange and Vanilla Crème Brûlée – £4.50

RECOMMENDED WALK

See recommendation on page 45.

 IMPORTANT FACTS

 LANDLORD
Alan Read

 CHEF
David Latter

 BREWERY/FREEHOUSE
Greene King

 FOOD SERVING TIMES
Lunch: Mon-Fri: 12-2.30pm, Sat-Sun: 12-5pm
Dinner: Mon-Sat 6-9.30pm

 NON-SMOKING AREA
Yes (restaurant entirely non-smoking)

 GARDEN
No (small patio)

 PARKING
No

 CHILDREN WELCOME
Yes

 DOGS ALLOWED
Yes (in bar only)

The Golden Pheasant
BURFORD

Silver Spoon
rating

High Street, Burford, Oxfordshire OX18 4QA
Tel: 01993 823223
www.goldenpheasant-burford.co.uk

Once you've experienced the glow of candles, comfy deep red chairs and a delicate rustic charm it will beckon you to open the oak door of The Golden Pheasant on Burford's famous High Street. A few steps more and the sight of Old Speckled Hen on tap and an almost always full restaurant is further gratification that you've made a wise choice.

Local chef Tim Jones is cooking good food here, and though the menu is somewhat meaty (with only one fish and one vegetarian main course, when I visited) the duck, hock of ham and rib-eye steak make you glad of being a carnivore. There are basic areas on the food front, however, that could be improved before 'food heaven' can be claimed. The salad garnishes were wilting by the time they were served and the carrots on the side-vegetables had been stewed more than granny's tea. Not to forget that when you're paying £14 for a wedge of Aberdeen Angus, an offer of a pepper mill is always appreciated.

And this is one area where The Golden Pheasant lets itself down a little: service. Some of the waiting staff are positively delightful, but others would be better employed at the nearest service station, not in this pub's proud surroundings. The popularity of the restaurant means you will probably have to pour your own wine and ask for more bread, but the congenial ambience tends to make up for minor shortcomings like this.

When in Burford, this Pub is certainly worth a visit. With more attention to detail in the busy kitchen and among some of the service staff, this pub could become better and better.

HOW TO GET THERE

On the A40 between Oxford and Cheltenham. Turn into Burford High Street and The Pheasant is half way down on the right hand side.

TYPICAL MENU AND PRICES

Starters

Homemade Chicken and Liver Pate – £5.45

Goats Cheese Tart with Roasted Peppers – £4.45

Main Courses

16oz Chargrilled Rib-Eye Steak – £13.95

Pan Fried Duck Breast with Plum and Brandy Sauce – £12.95

Desserts

Dark Chocolate Torte with Ice Cream – £4.95

Pannatone and Saffron Bread and Butter Pudding – £4.95

RECOMMENDED WALK

See recommendation on page 45.

 IMPORTANT FACTS

 LANDLORD
Martin Lyall

 CHEF
Tim Jones

 BREWERY/FREEHOUSE
Greene King

 FOOD SERVING TIMES
Lunch: Mon-Fri: 12-3pm,
Sat-Sun: 12-9pm
Dinner: Mon-Fri: 6.30-9pm,
Sat-Sun: 12-9pm

 NON-SMOKING AREA
Yes

 GARDEN
No (rear patio)

 PARKING
Yes

 CHILDREN WELCOME
Yes

 DOGS ALLOWED
Yes

The Fox Inn
GREAT BARRINGTON

Great Barrington, Burford, Oxfordshire OX18 4TB
Tel: 01451 844385
www.foxinnbarrington.co.uk

The Fox at Great Barrington will appeal to traditionalists who like to order unpretentious food straight from the blackboard and have their cutlery rolled up in green paper napkins. And unsurprisingly it's another pub in the Donnington stable. Its slightly run-down interior actually provides much of its character and brings back memories of yesteryear. The bar staff are friendly but, and please forgive me if this sounds overly fussy, your food might arrive after they have spent the last few minutes tickling the pub dog's ears.

The menu leans towards British classics such as Famous Fox Inn beef and ale pie, and sausage, mash, onions and gravy, but also offers continental favourites like carbonara. The chef makes good use of local produce too, with Cotswold jugged hare and Cotswold pork and chive sausage regularly on the menu. Puddings also stick to the tried and tested (and arteries) with favourites such as apple crumble, and treacle tart.

One appealing aspect of the Fox is the separate non-smoking restaurant at the rear, but if you're visiting mid-week you may find it a little lifeless and then that means eating in the smoky bar. The pub's position, right next to the winding Windrush, is also a draw. On a warm summer's evening it's satisfying to sip a Donnington Ale while eating trout fished from the very same river. It's an experience only slightly blighted by the waterside mushrooming of pub umbrellas.

The Ritz The Fox most certainly is not, but is doesn't pretend to be either. If you want home-cooked food that won't set your taste buds alight but will satisfy a healthy appetite then dinner by the river should not disappoint.

HOW TO GET THERE

Get on the A40, and Great Barrington is on the right hand side about two miles west of Burford en route to Cheltenham.

TYPICAL MENU AND PRICES

Starters

Creamy Garlic Mushrooms with Bread – £4.95

Cornish Crab and Salmon Cakes – £6.50

Main Courses

Beef and Ale Pie – £9.95

Sausage and Mash – £9.95

Desserts

Apple Crumble – £4.50

Treacle Tart – £4.50

RECOMMENDED WALK

There are a number of easy loops to choose from here. My preference would be to walk a few miles to Windrush village, down to Windrush Mill and then back for another Donnington to cool off. Walk duration: one hour.

 IMPORTANT FACTS

 LANDLORD
Paul Porter

 CHEF
Melony Simpson

 BREWERY/FREEHOUSE
Donnington

 FOOD SERVING TIMES
Lunch: Mon-Fri: 12-2.30pm,
Sat-Sun: 12-9.30pm
Dinner: Mon-Fri: 6.30-9.30pm

 NON-SMOKING AREA
Yes

 GARDEN
Yes

P **PARKING**
Yes

 CHILDREN WELCOME
Yes

 DOGS ALLOWED
Yes

The Inn For All Seasons
THE BARRINGTONS

The Barringtons, Burford, Oxfordshire OX18 4TN
Tel: 01451 844324
www.innforallseasons.com

The pub certainly lives up to its name, being a grand old ivy-clad Georgian coaching inn on the A40 specialising in seafood. And I can't rave about the seafood enough. Most days you'll find daily fresh squid, prawns, mussels, scallops and a range of whole fish. Chef and owner, Matthew Sharp, cooks with a distinct French influence, loading the seafood with herbs, sauces and fine touches that make the crustaceans look kings of the sea.

Once inside, the shiny original flagstones and inglenooks in each corner whisk you back in time. There's a snug bar offering mouthwatering cask ales including an exceptional pint of Cornish Sharp's Own (nothing to do with the chef).

Candlelit oak tables, mood lighting and fine polished cutlery all make the ambience inviting and slightly regal, yet relaxing.

The mussels in garlic and cream were plump and succulent. The whole lemon sole comes piping hot, cooked and garnished to perfection, and with a chilled half bottle of Chablis you're in seventh heaven. Marvellous.

Unfortunately Matthew might be an excellent cook, but he's a lousy DJ. I nearly had a course of brain as it oozed out my ears to what must have been called, 'The Most Depressing Songs of the 80s', complete with 10cc's 'I'm not in love'. Whatever happened to a bit of jazz or even some uplifting classical?

The serving staff are amiable and try hard, but obviously have not been given any proper training. Rudimentary queries of the reasonably extensive wine list are met with puzzled looks and the time lag between main course and accompanying vegetables was too long. If I was just rating food, then this roadside inn would be among the top of the pile. Change the music and spend a few hours briefing the staff and I'd be a frequent visitor.

HOW TO GET THERE
On the A40, just outside Burford, en route to Cheltenham.

TYPICAL MENU AND PRICES

Starters

Feta and Olive Salad with Pesto – £5.75

Gravlax with Sweet Dill Mustard – £5.95

Main Courses

Whole Lemon Sole – £16.50

Wild Mushroom and Fennel Risotto – £9.50

Desserts

Blackberry and Cassis Mousse – £4.75

Summer Pudding with Clotted Cream – £4.75

RECOMMENDED WALK

Take the nearby footpath leading to the two picturesque villages of the Barringtons and wander along the River Windrush stopping for a pint by the river at the Fox. Walking time: half an hour there, a little longer on the way back.

? IMPORTANT FACTS

 LANDLORD
Matthew & Heather Sharp

 CHEF
Matthew Sharp

 BREWERY/FREEHOUSE
Freehouse

 FOOD SERVING TIMES
Lunch: Mon-Sat:12-2.30pm, Sun: 12-2pm
Dinner: 6.30-9.30pm

 NON-SMOKING AREA
Yes (all non-smoking)

 GARDEN
Yes

 PARKING
Yes

 CHILDREN WELCOME
Yes

 DOGS ALLOWED
Yes (but only in the bar)

The Wheatsheaf Inn
NORTHLEACH

West End, Northleach, Gloucestershire GL54 3EZ
Tel: 01451 860244
www.wheatsheafatnorthleach.com

Northleach doesn't have the hustle and bustle that its nearby cousins Stow and Burford have, and this is also true of its pubs, which are on the quiet side during the week. Just a few hundred yards from the centre of this ancient wool town is the attractive Wheatsheaf Inn, a 17th century coaching inn that serves good food and beer in comfortable surroundings. It also offers extensive accommodation.

There is a daily blackboard serving the freshest seasonal ingredients. The small, wooden-floored restaurant leans toward contemporary English cooking with offerings that include fishcakes with chilli, lamb with lentils, steaks, and risotto. In terms of presentation, the asparagus with Parma ham in a hollandaise sauce caught my eye and was delightful.

It's worth noting that if you're planning a celebration, The Wheatsheaf sports a splendid long central dining table that seats 12.

Being a free house, there is always a range of guest beers on offer. The wine list serves the standard 10 whites and 10 reds with a few token roses. A total of eight wines are offered by the glass. Service is provided by local girls from the village who are friendly and able, but lack confidence in their art. Again, a little training might go a long way. No Silver Spoon for this pub, but it's certainly the best food pub in Northleach.

HOW TO GET THERE
Just off the A429 between Cirencester and Stow-on-the-Wold. Turn into Northleach and The Wheatsheaf is on your left half a mile after leaving the A429.

TYPICAL MENU AND PRICES

Starters

Salmon and Cod Fishcakes with Red Chilli
– £6.95

Poached Pear and Walnut Salad with Oxford
Blue – £5.50

Main Courses

Asparagus and Herb Risotto – £12.00

Roast End of Lamb with Lentils – £14.50

Desserts

Black Cherry and Almond Tart – £4.50

Fresh Strawberries and Cream – £4.95

RECOMMENDED WALK

Monarch's Way and Diamond Way pierce the
centre of town, providing walkers with a number
of wonderful circular walking options that will
have you back in the market square to quench
your thirst within an hour-and-a-half.

 IMPORTANT FACTS

 LANDLORD
Gavin Harvard

 CHEF
Thomas Scurr

 BREWERY/FREEHOUSE
Freehouse

 FOOD SERVING TIMES
Lunch: 12-3pm
Dinner: 7-9.30pm

 NON-SMOKING AREA
Yes (all non-smoking)

 GARDEN
Yes

 PARKING
Yes

 CHILDREN WELCOME
Yes

 DOGS ALLOWED
Yes

The Puesdown Inn
COMPTON ABDALE

Silver Spoon rating

Compton Abdale, Gloucestershire GL54 4DN
Tel: 01451 860262
www.puesdown.cotswoldinns.com

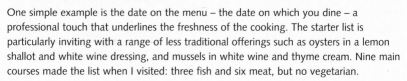

Walking up to The Puesdown Inn is at once inviting, but at the same time you can't help feeling that it's too cute and a little old lady is inside making children into ginger bread. But the magic inside has been brought by the owners who have travelled the world working in some of the finest hotels.

One simple example is the date on the menu – the date on which you dine – a professional touch that underlines the freshness of the cooking. The starter list is particularly inviting with a range of less traditional offerings such as oysters in a lemon shallot and white wine dressing, and mussels in white wine and thyme cream. Nine main courses made the list when I visited: three fish and six meat, but no vegetarian.

The food is of a very high standard and leans toward the nouveau with some intriguing fusion on offer, some which work well, others not so. The chef clearly enjoys experimenting and probably has Heston Blumenthal pictures hanging on the kitchen wall. As is common with this type of cuisine, the portions can seem mean for lovers of traditional pub food, but that's not the target market of the Puesdown.

There's a wonderful garden at the rear where you can enjoy excellent desserts or a glass of wine. There's an unusually well-priced wine list which offsets the slightly overpriced food. The owners have come up with an innovative wine offering, whereby any bottle under £20 can be bought by the glass, and that's 90% of the wines on offer.

This is a rather good pub, excellent for a celebration or just something refreshing and new. It's not for the traditionalist in search of roast beef and Yorkshire pudding, with all-you-can-eat roast tatties. Nor is it for someone whose credit card has been cut up.

HOW TO GET THERE
On the A40 between Cheltenham and Burford.

TYPICAL MENU AND PRICES

Starters

Soup of the Day – £5.00

Grilled Goat's Cheese with Rocket Salad – £6.00

Main Courses

Chargrilled Scottish Salmon – £15.00

Chicken Breast, Wild Mushrooms and Herb Pasta – £15.00

Desserts

Chocolate Tart with White Chocolate Sorbet – £4.95

Crème Brûlée – £4.95

RECOMMENDED WALK

A footpath alongside and at the rear of the Puesdown takes you to the Diamond Way over beautiful countryside to the village of Turkdean, and will loop you round to your starting point in around an hour-and-a-half.

 IMPORTANT FACTS

 LANDLORD
John & Maggie Armstrong

 CHEF
John Armstrong

 BREWERY/FREEHOUSE
Freehouse

 FOOD SERVING TIMES
Lunch: Mon-Thurs: 12-3pm
Dinner: Mon-Thurs: 6-10.30pm,
Fri-Sun: 12-10.30pm

 NON-SMOKING AREA
Yes

 GARDEN
Yes

 PARKING
Yes

 CHILDREN WELCOME
Yes

 DOGS ALLOWED
Yes (on a lead)

The Green Dragon Inn
COCKLEFORD

Silver Spoon rating

Cockleford, Near Cowley, Cheltenham, Gloucestershire
GL53 9NW Tel: 01242 870271
www.green-dragon-inn.co.uk

Any pub serving chargrilled Tiger prawns on the starter menu is worth further inspection. And inspectors of this little gem, tucked away in glorious Gloucestershire countryside, won't be disappointed. It's busy, but service is excellent. It has a contemporary feel, but all the old world charms remain. The cooking is modern, but rustic simplicity is at its core.

There are three intimate eating areas on polished flagstones cobbled around two busy bars. Low-beamed, wonky ceilings and large open fireplaces make it a cosy affair at any time of the year. There's a large eating area in the front, which is perfect on a sunny day. Diners can tuck into a varied cheese board and nurse a bottle of Chardonnay, or those succulent Tiger prawns, followed by pan-fried Snapper fillet, all of which will have gastronomic taste buds in a whirl.

Real ales include Hook Norton and a rather good pint of Buttcombe. Eighteen wines adorn the varied wine list of which seven come by the glass and all with useful detailed descriptions of flavours for the novice to choose from.

An unpretentious but well-heeled crowd flock here and for good reason. Even though it may sound like a Chinese restaurant in west London, The Green Dragon Inn is anything but.

HOW TO GET THERE
Five miles south of Cheltenham on the A435, look for signs to Cockleford and turn right.

TYPICAL MENU AND PRICES

Starters

Warm Salad of Brie and Bacon – £5.50

Chargrilled Rack of Tiger Prawns – £6.00

Main Courses

Thai Green Curry – £10.00

Pan-fried Red Snapper Fillet – £12.00

Desserts

Banoffee Pie – £4.50

Apricot and Almond Crumble – £4.50

RECOMMENDED WALK

Cowley Wood is just outside the front door.
Use the footpath to walk round it or through it.
Distances vary depending on your route
preference.

Note: Use OS Explorer 179 for Cockleford.

 IMPORTANT FACTS

 LANDLORD
Simon & Nicola Haly

 CHEF
Simon Haly

 BREWERY/FREEHOUSE
Freehouse

 **FOOD SERVING TIMES**
Lunch: 12-2.30pm
Dinner: 6-10pm

 NON-SMOKING AREA
Yes

 GARDEN
Yes

 PARKING
Yes

 CHILDREN WELCOME
Yes

 DOGS ALLOWED
Yes (on a lead)

The Butcher's Arms
SHEEPSCOMBE

Sheepscombe, nr Painswick, Gloucestershire GL6 7RH
Tel: 01452 812113
www.cotswoldinns.co.uk

Fine ales and outstanding views are the two main reasons for trekking to The Butcher's Arms at Sheepscombe. It's not for the food, however. The food isn't bad, it's just dull pub food that needs some passion and thought thrown into the pan.

Many pubs south of Cirencester have not yet fully caught onto to the food renaissance running wild in the northern Cotswolds and the Butcher's Arms is one such pub. It would help remove the take-away feel if things like the pepper and salt sachets were banned from the outside tables, and fresh salt and pepper mills were introduced to season one's food.

Imagination is sadly lacking on the food front. The lunch menu serves a range of rolls, wraps, bagels and salads and there are also the usual pub grub suspects, such as scampi, rump steaks, and, wait for it, that old 70s favourite, gammon steaks with pineapple chunks!

The Arms itself is worthy of being called a classic pub, however, as it does have bags of country character and serves fine cask ale, which includes the excellent and unusually named Dorothy Goodbody: good body by name and good body by taste, too. The beautiful views on a sunny day are also worth driving from afar to savour. Worth a visit for sure, but not if you're looking for a gastronomic feast.

HOW TO GET THERE
Five miles north of Stroud on the B4070, turn left for Sheepscombe.

TYPICAL MENU AND PRICES

Starters

Blanched Whitebait – £5.25

Field Mushroom topped with Tomato and Mozzarella – £5.50

Main Courses

Pork Chop Braised with Potatoes – £8.75

Cod and Chips – £8.25

Desserts

Fruit Crumbles – £4.25

Bread and Butter Pudding – £4.25

RECOMMENDED WALK

You're spoilt for choice here, with any number of walks in any direction. A nice short walk would be to take the signed footpaths to the charming small town of Painswick. Half a mile up the road from Painswick you'll find Rococo Garden (www.rococogarden.co.uk), which I hear is very nice.

Note: Use OS Explorer 179 for Sheepscombe.

 IMPORTANT FACTS

 LANDLORD
Johnny & Hilary Johnston

 CHEF
Merin Petre

 BREWERY/FREEHOUSE
Freehouse

 FOOD SERVING TIMES
Lunch: 12-2.30pm
Dinner: 7-9.30pm

 NON-SMOKING AREA
Yes (all non-smoking)

 GARDEN
Yes

 PARKING
Yes

 CHILDREN WELCOME
Yes

 DOGS ALLOWED
No (but allowed in garden)

The Seven Tuns
CHEDWORTH

Silver Spoon rating

Queen Street, Chedworth,
Gloucestershire GL54 4AE
Tel: 01285 720242

If you take an immediate right after the Fossebridge Inn going southbound toward Cirencester on the A429, you will drive through some of the most stunning Cotswold countryside you are likely to set eyes on. Keep going a winding three miles and you'll arrive in one of England's longest villages: Chedworth. It's a bit of a stretch from one end of the village to the other made worse by there being only one pub in town: the 17th century Tudor-beamed Seven Tuns.

Now, if you're interested in the paranormal you'll be right at home here. There are said to be ghosts floating around and one trip up the stairs to the skittle alley and even the most sceptical will find the trip unnerving. Chills running up the old backbone and so on.

Being a Young's pub you will be treated to some superb beers including the very drinkable, honey-fused draught Waggledance. Candlelit rustic tables, low ceilings and a good crowd of locals whet the appetite for the cooking.

Mussels were on the menu on the day I dined here and they tasted as fresh as if you had eaten them dockside in Cornwall from where they came. Wiltshire ham with egg and chips is also a fine treat. Other main courses to choose from include sausage and mash, smoked haddock, carbonara, fish and chips, and steak – all safe, comforting and filling.

The service can be slow when it's near full, but with great ales and good food while on ghost watch, it's all fun and a trip to The Seven Tuns is a must.

HOW TO GET THERE
Six miles north of Cirencester on the A429, hang a left when you see signs for Chedworth.

TYPICAL MENU AND PRICES

Starters

Tomato and Mozzarella with Pesto – £4.95

Parma Ham, Fig and Honey Salad – £5.95

Main Courses

Wiltshire Ham, Egg and Chips – £7.95

Fish and Chips – £8.95

Desserts

Apple and Toffee Crumble – £4.50

Strawberries and Cream – £4.50

RECOMMENDED WALK

It's said to be the longest village in England, so just a walk through it would give you a reasonable cardiovascular work-out. There is, of course, the nearby National Trust property, Chedworth Roman Villa, deep within Chedworth woods. Monarch's Way will lead you there within an hour.

 IMPORTANT FACTS

 LANDLORD
Alex Davenport-Jones

 CHEF
Fred Davenport-Jones & Alex Broughton

 **BREWERY/FREEHOUSE**
Youngs

 FOOD SERVING TIMES
Lunch: Mon-Fri: 12-2.30pm, Sat-Sun: 12-3pm
Dinner: Mon-Sat: 6.30-9.30pm, Sun: 6.30-9pm

 NON-SMOKING AREA
Yes

 GARDEN
Yes

 PARKING
Yes

 CHILDREN WELCOME
Yes

 DOGS ALLOWED
Yes

The Fossebridge Inn
FOSSEBRIDGE

Silver Spoon
rating

Fossebridge, Nr Cheltenham,
Gloucestershire GL54 3JS Tel: 01285 720721
www.fossebridgeinn.co.uk

Although the Cotswolds can lay claim to providing England with the source of the River Thames, the one thing the area does lack is pubs alongside a wide expanse of flowing river. Sat Thames-side in Royal Berkshire on a late summer's day with a pint of Brakspear in hand is truly one of life's great joys. About as good as it gets in the Cotswolds is the Fossebridge Inn, providing a rare chance to dine and drink by the much smaller River Coln.

Fossebridge is wedged into a dramatic valley carved by the Coln on the A429 between Cirencester and Stow. As with most roadside pubs, it's tempting to drive on by in search of something more secluded, but that would be a mistake.

The pub has an enormous west-facing, rear garden that sits alongside the river and, if the weather permits, it is perfect for al fresco lunch or dinner. Inside, this grand old place has lots of charm and has many of its old features retained in the battered stone and woodwork.

I'm not one for generalising but the ears do stand up when you hear a Frenchman running through the menu, dressed in spoiled whites. Head chef, Guillery Laurant, has been cooking in pubs for years and his cooking is everything you'd expect from a Frenchman: simple, stylish and fresh.

On a fine day, sitting by the rolling river, listening to the birds (and the cars on the A429), this would be my choice to bring the family for lunch on the lawn.

HOW TO GET THERE

On the A429 between Cirencester and Northleach.

TYPICAL MENU AND PRICES

Starters

Whitebait with Paprika Mayonnaise – £5.50

Glazed Chicken Liver and Smoked Bacon Salad – £5.95

Main Courses

Pan-fried Haddock with Chips – £8.95

Pan-fried Chicken Breast with Asparagus and Tarragon – £11.85

Desserts

Tiramisu and Ice Cream – £4.50

Cheese and Biscuits – £5.95

RECOMMENDED WALK

Turn right outside the pub entrance and then pick up the footpath signs on your right shortly thereafter and you will be taken along some of the most glorious Cotswold countryside you are likely to see, leading to Chedworth. Though only approximately three miles away there are some steep hills in between, making a pint of Young's at The Seven Tuns even more gratifying than normal.

 IMPORTANT FACTS

 LANDLORD
Robert Jenkins

 CHEF
Guillery Laurant

 BREWERY/FREEHOUSE
Freehouse

 FOOD SERVING TIMES
Lunch: Mon-Sun: 12-3pm
Dinner: Mon-Sat: 6.30-10pm,
Sun: 7-9.30pm

 NON-SMOKING AREA
Yes

 GARDEN
Yes

 PARKING
Yes

 CHILDREN WELCOME
Yes

 DOGS ALLOWED
Yes

The Hare & Hounds Inn
FOSSE CROSS

Silver Spoon rating

Fosse Cross, Nr Chedworth,
Gloucestershire GL54 4NN
Tel: 01285 720288

A well-positioned speed camera is almost opposite The Hare & Hounds and is one good reason to slow down, pull over and duck into this beautiful roadside pub, which keeps excellent Arkells Ales and serves high quality food.

The 15th century building has been lovingly restored and retains all the old features of beamed ceilings, timber floors and fireplaces in each corner. There's plenty of parking and a decent-sized beer garden to the side.

French chef, Guillery Laurant from the nearby Fossebridge Inn, eats here and that's a good recommendation. The menu is contemporary cooking, with a bent towards local fresh ingredients. The locally-caught trout and locally-made goats cheese are exquisite and Gloucester Old Spot sausages often make the daily specials' board.

The Italian landlord and chef, Geraldo Ragosa, has a touch of the nouvelle cuisine in his presentation and portions, in other words small and fancy. My samosas arrived in filo pastry, on a neatly crafted rectangular potato bed, criss-crossed with a sweet chilli sauce – very pretty and most tasty, but I needed more.

The wine list is also good, with over thirty to choose from. The classic New Zealand Cloudy Bay Sauvignon is well priced for a pub at £29.95 and there are some fine French reds to tease your taste buds. A great little pub that seems not to have been truly discovered – yet!

HOW TO GET THERE
On the A429 between Cirencester and Northleach.

TYPICAL MENU AND PRICES

Starters

Coln Valley Smoked Trout – £6.50

Deep-fried Cerney Goats Cheese – £5.95

Main Courses

Wild Mushroom and Sun-dried Tomato Risotto – £12.95

Pan-fried Plaice with Spinach in Peppercorn Sauce – £15.50

Desserts

Meringue, Cream and Fruit – £4.95

Raspberry and Mascarpone Cheesecake – £4.95

RECOMMENDED WALK

Fosse Cross is a little isolated, making walking options limited. My recommendation would be to drive to nearby Chedworth and pick up any number of magnificent trails there.

 IMPORTANT FACTS

 LANDLORD
Geraldo & Angela Ragosa

 CHEF
Geraldo Ragosa

 BREWERY/FREEHOUSE
Arkells

 FOOD SERVING TIMES
Lunch: Mon-Sat: 12-2.30pm, Sun: 12-3pm
Dinner: Mon-Sat: 6.30-9.30pm, Sun: 7-9pm

 NON-SMOKING AREA
Yes

 GARDEN
Yes

 PARKING
Yes

 CHILDREN WELCOME
Yes

 DOGS ALLOWED
Yes

The Swan at Southrop
SOUTHROP

Silver Spoon rating

Southrop, Lechlade, Gloucestershire GL7 3NU
Tel: 01367 850205
www.theswanatsouthrop.co.uk

The Swan has become the focal point of an otherwise sleepy, if pretty, village on the south-eastern edges of the Cotswolds. Only the ivy-smothered dry-stone walls outside this fine Georgian establishment remind you that you're in the Cotswolds, as the quality of food and service inside this little gem is London 'fine dining' at its very best.

Furniture straight from the Antiques Roadshow, along with works of art displayed as in Bond Street, and an interior design of which Sir Terence Conran himself no doubt approved (he's a business partner of the owner), all make the experience at The Swan one to fondly remember.

Food is intelligent, yet simple and excellent in every way. The menu changes daily and is cooking creativity at its very best. I was served impeccable fish soup with rouille, gruyere and croutons. My cold baked ham with eggs and chips was positively uplifting. As well as local guest ales, there is a mouth-watering wine list with almost 60 wines to choose from; prices start at £16.50 a bottle.

Fine detail is everywhere. The phone ring evokes memories of the old bakelite set your Granny would have had. The staff are friendly, knowledgeable, well-trained and on time, without being constantly on your shoulder. It's hard to find fault with The Swan: they have created a little bit of magic in this small corner of The Cotswolds, and long may they be successful.

HOW TO GET THERE

A few miles off the A361 not far from Lechlade. Not brilliantly signposted, but the only pub in town.

TYPICAL MENU AND PRICES

Starters

Cream of Leek Soup – £4.50

Chicken Liver and Foie Gras Pate – £7.50

Main Courses

Cold Baked Ham with Fried Eggs and Chips – £7.50

Linguine with Ricotta, Olives and Cherry Tomatoes – £8.50

Desserts

Raspberry Sorbet – £4.00

Hot Chocolate Fondant with Vanilla Ice Cream – £4.00

RECOMMENDED WALK

There is a maze of footpaths in and around Southrop that twist and turn over the River Leach. Keener walkers will revel in the longer walk southwards along the Leach toward Lechlade, where the river empties into the beautiful Horseshoe Lake.

 IMPORTANT FACTS

 LANDLORD
Graham Williams

 CHEF
James Parkinson

 BREWERY/FREEHOUSE
Freehouse

 FOOD SERVING TIMES
Lunch: Mon-Fri: 12-2.30pm, Sat-Sun: 12-3.30pm
Dinner: Mon-Sat: 7-10pm, Sun: 7-9pm

 NON-SMOKING AREA
Yes

 GARDEN
No

 PARKING
No

 CHILDREN WELCOME
Yes

 DOGS ALLOWED
Yes (in the bar only)

The New Inn
COLN ST-ALDWYNS

Coln St-Aldwyns, Nr Cirencester, Gloucestershire GL7 5AN
Tel: 01285 750651
www.new-inn.co.uk

It sounds like a village on the north shore of Cornwall and it gets mobile phone reception like the north shore of Cornwall, but in fact Coln St Aldwyn nestles in stunning rural Gloucestershire.

The deception continues since The New Inn is anything but, dating back to the 16th century. It's a typical country inn with no airs and graces, but not many surprises either. You can eat at the bar, which is pleasant enough if you're allergic to sunlight, but then that does well in covering a need of a spring clean. The dining room is brighter and rather delightful: it's non-smoking but only open in the evenings, and for Sunday lunch.

This Free House was taken over by the Scottish/Taiwanese partnership of Roger and Angela Kimmett and they offer an internationally varied menu, ranging from curries to steaks and inventive vegetarian dishes. There's a daily blackboard menu that seems to have something for everyone and light bar snacks, including baguettes with different fillings.

Thankfully there are local ales that include Hook Norton, Archers and Wadworths. The wine list is extensive, varied and covers all budgets.

Perhaps my palate was getting over-used to subtle tastes, but the balsamic vinegar was certainly held over my mixed leaves and goats cheese salad for a few seconds too long. But this shouldn't stop you from coming to the relaxing New Inn. I would, however, recommend the garden if it's warm enough, or the dining-room for dinner, rather than the bar.

HOW TO GET THERE

Between Cirencester and Burford you'll see Bibury on the B4425. Look for signposts to Coln St Aldwyns from there.

TYPICAL MENU AND PRICES

Starters

Greek Salad – £5.95

Smoked Salmon with Caperberries – £7.50

Main Courses

Poached Salmon, Salad and New Potatoes – £9.95

Lamb Madras with Pilau Rice – £10.25

Desserts

Sticky Toffee Pudding – £5.25

Cherry Crème Brûlée – £5.25

RECOMMENDED WALK

The owner of the New Inn enjoyed the walking so much around Coln that he bought himself a pub here. It's not hard to see why. There are a number of footpaths and bridleways criss-crossing the River Coln and that link to the nearby villages of Hatherop and Quenington, all within a mile of one another.

? IMPORTANT FACTS

 LANDLORD
Roger & Angela Kimmett

 CHEF
Not prepared to say

 BREWERY/FREEHOUSE
Freehouse

 FOOD SERVING TIMES
Lunch: Mon-Fri: 12-2pm, Sat-Sun: 12-2.30pm
Dinner: Mon-Fri: 7-9pm, Sat-Sun: 7-9.30pm

 NON-SMOKING AREA
Yes

 GARDEN
Yes

 PARKING
Yes

 CHILDREN WELCOME
Yes

 DOGS ALLOWED
Yes

The Village Inn Pub
BARNSLEY

Barnsley, Cirencester, Gloucestershire GL7 5EF
Tel: 01285 740421
www.thevillagepub.co.uk

Silver Spoon rating

No, I haven't lifted something from a Yorkshire guide to pubs by mistake. Barnsley in Gloucestershire is a somewhat quainter than its northern sister and is a few fields away from quintessentially English, Bibury. This is one of my favourite pubs. It's inviting, the service is excellent and the food created by Pierro Boi (English of Italian descent) is faultless.

The owners have turned The Village Inn into a haven for fresh local food served in contemporary Cotswold surroundings. A labyrinth of snugs and rooms branch off from the bar, all with low-beamed wonky ceilings, flagstoned floors and large open fireplaces.

Pull up a chair and you'll soon be presented with a menu-of-the-day which will reflect what's fresh and in season. I had the positively delightful roast turbot on a bed of mash and spinach, washed down with a half of Hook Norton. I followed this with warm pecan pie with fresh cream and began looking at my diary to see when I could fix a time to come back for more.

The landlord clearly takes his cellar seriously, with no less than 28 reds on offer, 17 of which are under £20 a bottle. There are 19 whites to choose from, starting at a reasonable £12 and going up to a more considered £35 for a bottle of Sancerre 2002. Five reds and five whites are offered by the glass.

There's a large open courtyard at the rear, and plenty of parking for the traveller. If you're ever near Cirencester and you hear your belly rumbling, you're in for a treat if you visit this village pub.

HOW TO GET THERE
On the B4425 four miles north-east of Cirencester.

TYPICAL MENU AND PRICES

Starters

Feta, Olive and Red Onion Salad – £6.50

Seared Mackerel with Potato and Bacon Salad – £6.50

Main Courses

Roast Salmon, Crushed Potato and Rocket – £14.50

Rib-Eye Steak with Roast Tomatoes and Mushroom – £17.25

Desserts

Custard & Rhubarb Tart – £6.00

Pecan Pie with Cream – £6.00

RECOMMENDED WALK

The obvious walk from here is north east along bridleways and footpaths to beautiful Bibury and the river Coln. Barnsley to Bibury and back again will chalk up around six or seven miles over open countryside and take around an hour and half.

IMPORTANT FACTS

 LANDLORD
Rupert Pendred

 CHEF
Pierro Boi

 BREWERY/FREEHOUSE
Freehouse

 FOOD SERVING TIMES
Lunch: Mon-Fri: 12-2.30pm, Sat-Sun: 12-3pm
Dinner: Sun-Thurs: 7-9.30pm, Fri-Sat: 7-10pm

 NON-SMOKING AREA
Yes

 GARDEN
Yes

 PARKING
Yes

 CHILDREN WELCOME
Yes

 DOGS ALLOWED
Yes

The Bell at Sapperton
SAPPERTON

Silver Spoon rating

Nr. Cirencester, Gloucestershire GL7 6LE
Tel: 01285 760298
www.foodatthebell.co.uk

The website address sums it up –
foodatthebell.co.uk. If you've ever had the
pleasure of visiting South Africa, you'll know that
they have some mouthwatering specialities, have
a particularly fine eye for meat and seafood and
can compete with the best chefs worldwide. Paul Davidson and Pat LeJeune have
exported a little piece of Capetonian magic to within the Cotswold stone walls of The
Bell at Sapperton.

Gordon Ramsey would be hard-pressed to find fault in Ivan Reid's kitchen. The flavours,
presentation, serving portions, timing – it's all perfect. The menu changes each month
and the specials' board changes daily. And add to that the produce is overwhelmingly
local. A delight.

To accompany the fine food is an extensive wine list for all budgets and regular guest
beers. And for those who may consider more regular visits, the landlord will charge a
small handling fee to allow storage of your own wine in his cellar.

There are a lot of tasteful contemporary touches of lighter wood and leather that manage
to complement the ancient interior. There are four inviting dining areas, fireplaces,
exposed beams, candles, fresh flowers – nothing is left to chance. Service is all South
African too, and that means it's top-notch; professional and friendly – just as it should be.
I can't recommend The Bell highly enough. It's worth driving a long way to get to, and
three Silver Spoons are awarded in praise.

HOW TO GET THERE
Take the A419 west from Cirencester. Look out for signs after four miles and turn right
into Sapperton.

TYPICAL MENU AND PRICES

Starters

Deep-fried Goats Cheese in a Herb Crust
– £6.95

Fresh Portland Crab tossed with Pesto – £8.00

Main Courses

Pan-fried Tenderloin of Old Spot Pork – £14.50

Breast of Chicken, Spiced Couscous and Feta
Cheese – £13.95

Desserts

Bakewell Tart and Clotted Cream – £5.75

Crème Brûlée with Roasted Apricots – £5.75

RECOMMENDED WALK

See recommendation on page 77.

Note: Use OS Explorer 168 for Sapperton.

? IMPORTANT FACTS

 LANDLORD
Paul Davidson &
Pat LeJeune

 CHEF
Ivan Reid

 BREWERY/FREEHOUSE
Freehouse

 FOOD SERVING TIMES
Lunch: 12-2pm
Dinner: 7-9.30pm

 NON-SMOKING AREA
Yes

 GARDEN
Yes

 PARKING
Yes

 CHILDREN WELCOME
Only in the afternoon

 DOGS ALLOWED
Yes

Crown Inn
FRAMPTON MANSELL

Frampton Mansell, Stroud, Gloucestershire GL6 8JG
Tel: 01285 760601

If you're returning to England or you want to impress your American friends and are seeking a vision of "those green and pleasant lands", then visit the Crown Inn. The landscape wraps itself around this hostelry, with views from the beer garden across the Golden Valley that should silence any loud claims about 'Back home' from unappreciative visitors.

In the sophistication stakes, it gets beaten by a good furlong by the nearby Bell at Sapperton, but then it's not trying to be the Derby winner. Truthfully, any thoroughbred would have kicked the wittering juke box in the corner into next week's car boot sale. The service is creaky and the flowers on the tables were wilting, but even so the Crown Inn just about gets away with it because of its old charm and stunning location.

The food is fine: well-presented and it comes in generous portions. The menu is in keeping with the traditional setting and leans towards typical pub grub. There are also a few adventurous creations that seem to work well on the daily specials board.

No Silver Spoons here, but then if you're of the true pub fraternity, forget the food, grab a pint of Speckled Hen, sit outside and sup up the view.

HOW TO GET THERE

Roughly half way between Stroud and Cirencester on the A419, look out for signs to Frampton Mansell which is a few miles off the main road.

TYPICAL MENU AND PRICES

Starters

Soup of the Day – £4.95

Homemade Pork and Liver Pate – £5.00

Main Courses

Pan-seared Duck Breast with Brandy and Orange Sauce – £12.50

Chicken Tikka Masala with Rice – £8.95

Desserts

Strawberry Cheesecake – £4.50

Pineapple Sundae – £4.50

RECOMMENDED WALK

There's a good two-hour walk here that Landlord Shaun Davies at The White Horse uses regularly to keep himself fit. Over refreshments plot your route down to the railway line, look both ways, and continue on to the River Frome. From here you can take footpaths east or west along the river and loop back when you get tired. Warning: beautiful views means steep hills. Bring water, a compass and flares in case you conk out.

Note: Use OS Explorer 168 for Frampton Mansell.

? IMPORTANT FACTS

 LANDLORD
Philip Creed

 CHEF
Philip Creed

 BREWERY/FREEHOUSE
Freehouse

 FOOD SERVING TIMES
Lunch: 12-2.30pm
Dinner: Mon-Fri: 6.30-9.30pm,
Sat-Sun: 6.30-10pm

 NON-SMOKING AREA
Yes

 GARDEN
Yes

 PARKING
Yes

 CHILDREN WELCOME
Yes (in certain sections)

 DOGS ALLOWED
Yes

The White Horse
FRAMPTON MANSELL

Silver Spoon rating

Cirencester Road, Frampton Mansell,
Gloucestershire GL6 8HZ Tel: 01285 760960
www.cotswoldwhitehorse.com

Take a handful of 1960s concrete chic, add mock
Georgian windows, mix to the foundation of dirty
farmhouse render and a dollop of exquisite
Bladerunner piping and you've got The White
Horse.

Had the owners invested as much time and money into bringing the exterior of the
building up to the same standards as the Licensee has on the interior, the neighbouring
A419 would be backed up to Cirencester. As it is, the temptation to follow Dorothy on
down the road is overwhelming.

But wait: it's what's inside that counts. There's a tiny bar (more of a pre-dinner waiting
room) and a delightfully snug restaurant serving up rather good food. The menu changes
daily and reflects the catch in Cornwall the same day, while the cuts of meat are from
nearby butchers in Cirencester and Lechlade. The menu is compact with just six or seven
starters and the same number of mains. Even vegetarians are catered for here.

You could start with fresh crab with guacamole, tomato salsa and caviar, washed down
with a glass of young South African Sauvignon, then follow with grilled black bream or
whole grilled plaice with saffron and caper butter – perfect with Chardonnay. The food is
beautifully presented and the restaurant is small enough for staff to be attentive even
when busy.

This is the sort of pub that you'll happily recommend to friends for eating when next in
the Cotswolds, although you'd be put off from sitting in the garden with a beer due to
the complete absence of architectural or aesthetic values from the building.

HOW TO GET THERE
Roughly half way between Stroud and Cirencester on the A419 (you'll see the nice
pipework).

TYPICAL MENU AND PRICES

Starters

Tomato and Basil Soup – £3.95

Greek Salad – £5.75

Main Courses

Rib-eye Steak with Cracked Black Pepper Sauce – £15.25

Leek Risotto with Grilled Goats Cheese and Pesto – £10.95

Desserts

Warm Pecan Tart with Vanilla Ice Cream – £4.75

Chocolate and Coffee Crème Brûlée – £4.75

RECOMMENDED WALK

See recommendation on page 77.

IMPORTANT FACTS

 LANDLORD
Shaun & Emma Davis

 CHEF
Howard Matthews

 BREWERY/FREEHOUSE
Freehouse

 FOOD SERVING TIMES
Lunch: Mon-Sat: 12-2.30pm, Sun: 12-3pm
Dinner: Mon-Sat: 7-9.45pm

 NON-SMOKING AREA
Yes

 GARDEN
Yes

 PARKING
Yes

 CHILDREN WELCOME
Yes

 DOGS ALLOWED
Yes

The Tunnel House Inn
COATES

Tarlton Road, Coates, Nr Cirencester, Gloucestershire GL7 6PW
Tel: 01285 770280
www.tunnelhouse.com

This Inn has one distinct claim to fame: it's just about the nearest pub in England to the source of the River Thames (thirty minutes walk from the bar). There's also an old canal that you can wade in beside the pub and where the name Tunnel House is from.

Originally used to house workers to build and operate the canal, when Henry Ford innovated travel and the motor car became popular, the Tunnel House was turned into a pub shortly after World War II. Today, it is a curious mix of slightly tacky memorabilia in the main bar and a more conservatively decorated restaurant overlooking beautiful countryside.

You can order at the bar from a menu that seems to have every pub classic ever invented on it: whitebait, garlic bread, lasagna, beer-battered cod, sausage, mash, onions and gravy, but no Madras curry. There are also some more original inventions including warm duck salad with coriander, and seared swordfish with garlic and tarragon.

There's well-kept Archers or Pig's Ear (also cockney rhyme for beer) from the nearby Uley (pronounced you-lee) brewery which certainly challenges you to take a pint. There's a surprisingly good wine list that sports about 20 wines, mostly under £20 a bottle. Two house reds and two house whites sell for £11.50.

Service is reasonable, and the bangers and mash washed down with a pint of Archers overlooking open Cotswolds fields will have you quickly deciding that The Tunnel House is well worth the drive, or wade.

HOW TO GET THERE
Without doubt the most difficult pub to find in the entire book. Head for Coates (which is just a few miles west of Cirencester on the A419) and bring your mobile phone and call ahead from there.

TYPICAL MENU AND PRICES

Starters

Whitebait with Fresh Lemon – £5.95

Trout, Salmon and Spinach Terrine – £6.00

Main Courses

Beer-battered Cod with Steakhouse Chips – £8.95

8oz Sirloin Steak with Tomato, Mushrooms and Chips – £13.00

Desserts

Cotswold Ice Cream – £3.00

Chocolate Brownie – £4.50

RECOMMENDED WALK

The MacMillan Way and Monarch's Way intersect right outside this pub's front door. Take Monarch's Way southwards and then follow the signs for Thames Path. After about half-an-hour you'll come across a large stone. That's the source of England's most famous river, the River Thames. If you prefer wood to water, Hailey Wood is at the rear of the pub and the MacMillan Way cuts through the middle.

Note: Use OS Explorer 168 for Coates.

 IMPORTANT FACTS

 LANDLORD
Andrew Freeland & Rupert Longdon

 CHEF
Gavin Monroe

 BREWERY/FREEHOUSE
Freehouse

 FOOD SERVING TIMES
Lunch: 12-2.15pm
Dinner: Mon-Fri: 6.45-9.15pm, Sat-Sun: 6.45-9.30pm

 NON-SMOKING AREA
Yes (all non-smoking in restaurant)

 GARDEN
Yes

 PARKING
Yes

 **CHILDREN WELCOME**
Yes

DOGS ALLOWED
Yes

The Gumstool Inn
NEAR TETBURY

Silver Spoon rating

Nr Tetbury, Gloucestershire GL8 8YJ
Tel: 01666 890391
www.calcotmanor.co.uk

Set in 220 acres of the glorious Calcot Estate, this pub makes for a great stop whilst exploring the southern wolds. It's also an attractive halt if you want a pint of London Pride and your partner wants to do a few Yoga stretches in the estate's state-of-the-art spa complex.

This welcoming freehouse on the estate serves a range of fine ales, complemented by an equally fine, monthly changing menu, which also has the ubiquitous 'daily specials'. The food has a distinctly international flavour, to coin a phrase, reflecting the international jet-set that visit: there's grilled halloumi cheese, Spanish chorizo and even the hard-to-find Sichuan pepper is used to season one oriental dish.

Aside from the foreign taste-bud ticklers, there are also modern British classics such as braised and roasted ham hock with onion mash or spit-roasted lemon and thyme chicken. The desserts are modern, fresh English classics too.

However, the peculiarly named Gumstool does suffer somewhat from the modern design of the long, open bar, glaring wall-lights set off nicely by the staff burgundy polo shirts and finished by furnishings courtesy of the local pine factory. Classic country pub this is not, but if you're in search of good food served by friendly and efficient staff then the Gumstool is worth coming to, if only to send the pub disbelievers away to wrap their legs around their necks.

HOW TO GET THERE
Three miles west of Tetbury on the A4135.

TYPICAL MENU AND PRICES

Starters

Mushroom and Spinach Herb Pancake – £6.50

Grilled Brixham Sardines with Capers – £6.95

Main Courses

Roast Monkfish with Curried Mussels and Leeks – £12.25

Slow-braised Shoulder of Lamb – £12.95

Desserts

Lemon Meringue Pie – £4.75

Rice Pudding with Rhubarb Jam – £4.75

RECOMMENDED WALK

See recommendation on page 87.

Note: Use OS Explorer 168 for Tetbury.

 IMPORTANT FACTS

 LANDLORD
Richard Ball

 CHEF
Michael Croft

 BREWERY/FREEHOUSE
Freehouse

 FOOD SERVING TIMES
Lunch: Mon-Fri: 12-2pm
Dinner: Mon-Fri: 5.30-9.30pm,
Sat: 12-9.30pm, Sun: 12-9pm

 NON-SMOKING AREA
Yes (all not smoking)

 GARDEN
Yes

 PARKING
Yes

 CHILDREN WELCOME
Yes

 DOGS ALLOWED
No

Tipputs
NEAR NAILSWORTH

Tiltups End, Nailsworth, Gloucestershire GL6 0QE
Tel: 01453 832466

Silver Spoon rating

I've never liked the word 'gastro', it brings back memories of food poisoning in Indonesia and a dose of enteritis added to it. I prefer the word 'pubstro', a mixed breed of pub and bistro. Tipputs defines this word perfectly.

Set on the A46 you could easily drive on past this Cotswolds' building. It's not exactly inconspicuous, being grey, stolid and standing on its own, but it doesn't shout 'Eat here', either.

That's Tipputs' mistake. The food and service combine to offer the consumer a little bit of London chic served in the surroundings of an old Cotswold roadside inn.

Start with the hummus with red onion tomato salsa and warm pitta, follow it with delectable sea bass served on a Greek salad and wash that down with one of the seventeen whites on offer. If there's still room, order mocha tart for afters.

There's the choice of an intimate non-smoking dining room looking like a fairly recent refurbishment, or the busy bar which looks older with its wide polished timber floors, walls of glowing golden stone and rustic tables. Service is professional and friendly, and the staff are knowledgeable and keen to make recommendations just in case you don't know what tuna carpaccio is.

This is one of four pubs in this privately-owned local chain. I have it on good authority that Tipputs serves the best food of the lot and on the results of this visit I see no reason to challenge that opinion.

HOW TO GET THERE
Six miles south of Stroud on the A46, on the right hand side.

TYPICAL MENU AND PRICES

Starters

Hummus with Red Onion Tomato Salsa – £4.95

Tuna Carpaccio with Coriander and Rocket – £5.95

Main Courses

Sea Bass served on Greek Salad – £15.95

Grilled Pork Cutlet with Creamed Leeks – £13.25

Desserts

Chocolate Mocha Tart with Vanilla Ice Cream – £4.25

Mixed Berry Parfait with Fruit Coulis – £4.25

RECOMMENDED WALK

There are lots of walking options here. You can step outside the front door, cross the road and walk south-east or east on sign-posted paths that will have you back at your starting-point within the hour. Or you could drive up the A46 a few miles to Minchinhampton Common to let the dog off the lead, or have a round of golf.

Note: Use OS Explorer 168 for Nailsworth.

 IMPORTANT FACTS

 LANDLORD
Nick Beardsley

 CHEF
Jeremy White

 BREWERY/FREEHOUSE
Freehouse

 FOOD SERVING TIMES
Mon-Sun: 11-10pm (3-6pm Light Bites)

 NON-SMOKING AREA
Yes (separate non-smoking restaurant)

 **GARDEN**
Yes

 PARKING
Yes

 CHILDREN WELCOME
Yes

 DOGS ALLOWED
Yes (in main bar only)

The Trouble House
NEAR TETBURY

Silver Spoon rating

Nr Tetbury, Gloucestershire GL8 8SG
Tel: 01666 502206
www.troublehouse.co.uk

Believe it or not, a customer had his throat slit in this pub during the agricultural riots of the 1700s and the locals are still talking about it. It wasn't the Wadworths range of beers that started the disagreement, but the incident gave the pub its name. The tenants have also managed to get people talking about its food.

This typical roadside coaching inn has been lovingly restored to its former glory: the tables come in a variety of shapes and sizes, only managing a common 'rustic' between them, matching the low-beamed ceilings, glowing candles at dusk and homely fireplaces. The kitchen manages to be rustic too, and produces mind-blowingly good food.

Its nod to modernity is the choice of contemporary art and the magazine articles and newspaper cuttings that adorn the white-washed stone walls. The subject matter isn't about an ancient homicide, but doffs the editorial cap to the Michelin-starred culinary skills of the chef, Michael Bedford.

Michael's inventions have to be tasted to be fully appreciated as imagination might not go far enough to include spiced monkfish with dhal, roasted cod with smoked haddock chowder or crayfish cappuccino. A large majority of produce is organic and is from the nearby back-garden of Prince Charles' Highgrove Estate. Heaven. The food manages to be innovative and different, yet simple and tasty – it's a perfect formula that brings sighs of approval from a discerning clientele.

Be warned, there can be a long wait for food, but at least the staff tell you when you order. Besides, the food is so good that the waiting becomes irrelevant.

A three-course dinner for two, pre-dinner drinks and a bottle of wine around the £20 mark won't bring you much change from £100, but dining here is not just about having dinner, it's also about having a food experience that you're not likely to forget in a hurry.

HOW TO GET THERE
Just a couple of miles north of Tetbury on the A433.

TYPICAL MENU AND PRICES

Starters

Foie Gras and Apple Terrine – £8.25

Moules Mariniere – £6.95

Main Courses

Pure Bred Rib-eye Steak in Béarnaise Sauce – £16.50

Roasted Cod with Smoked Haddock Chowder – £16.25

Desserts

Creamed Rice Pudding with Poached Peaches – £5.25

Strawberry Pavlova – £5.25

RECOMMENDED WALK

Highgrove Estate wraps itself around the immediate countryside here and hence poking ones walking stick wherever one wants is not allowed. The best bet is to drive a few miles south to the renowned Westonbirt Arboretum. Open 365 days a year the arboretum's collection contains 18,000 trees and shrubs, covering 600 acres of Grade 1 listed landscape – a must see place in Autumn, and great for walks year round. Note: Use OS Explorer 168 for Tetbury.

 IMPORTANT FACTS

 LANDLORD
Michael & Sarah Bedford

 CHEF
Michael Bedford

 BREWERY/FREEHOUSE
Wadworths

 FOOD SERVING TIMES
Lunch: Tues-Sun: 12-2pm
Dinner: Tues-Sat: 7-9.30pm

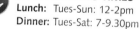 **NON-SMOKING AREA**
Yes

 GARDEN
Yes (small one)

 PARKING
Yes

 CHILDREN WELCOME
Yes

 DOGS ALLOWED
Yes

Feedback Please use block capitals

If by chance I have omitted a rare gem, feel free to tell me by returning this form, or emailing the details to lastorders@pukkapubs.com. If I am in agreement with you, I will publish it in the next edition.

Pub name:

Pub address:

Pub website:

Pub tel no:

What you liked:

What you didn't like:

Your name:

Your address:

Your e-mail:

Please post this feedback form to: PukkaPubs.com, PO Box 24, Stow-on-the-Wold, Cheltenham, GL54 1WX, England.